WILD and *Whirling* WORDS

ALSO BY H. L. HIX

POETRY

Surely As Birds Fly
Rational Numbers
Perfect Hell

ARTISTS' BOOKS AND LIMITED EDITIONS

This Translucent Tissue (artist's book by Judi Ross)
The Last Hour (artist's book by Egidijus Rudinskas)
Intellectual Pleasures (limited edition by Aralia Press)

TRANSLATION

City of Ash, by Eugenijus Ališanka, trans. with the author

ARTIST CATALOGS

Jason Pollen
Kyoung Ae Cho

THEORY AND CRITICISM

As Easy As Lying: Essays on Poetry*
Understanding William H. Gass
Understanding W. S. Merwin
Spirits Hovering Over the Ashes: Legacies of Postmodern Theory
Morte d'Author: An Autopsy

*Also published by Etruscan Press.

WILD and *Whirling* WORDS

•

A Poetic Conversation

•

MODERATED BY
H. L. HIX

etruscan press

Etruscan Press
P.O. Box 9685
Silver Spring, MD 20916-9685

www.etruscanpress.org

Publisher's Cataloging-in-Publication
(Provided by Quality Books, Inc.)
Wild and whirling words : a poetic conversation / moderated
  by H.L. Hix.
    p. cm.
    ISBN 0-9745995-0-6

    1. American poetry--21st century. 2. American poetry
  --21st century--History and criticism.   I. Hix, H. L.

PS617.W55 2004   811'.608
                           QB133-1646

Designed by Elizabeth Woll.

Contents

HORATIO: *These are but wild and whirling words, my lord.*

HAMLET: *I am sorry they offend you, heartily;*
Yes, faith, heartily.

HORATIO: *There's no offense, my lord.*

Preface

The book in your hands contains a colloquy unlike any held before. Its participants have made their conversation so rich and provocative that in this preface I count myself bound by the same imperative that should guide a conductor introducing a symphony to the orchestra's audience at an afternoon concert: orient us, if you must, with the circumstances of the piece's composition or a tip about something to listen for, but then shut up, turn around, and let the musicians do their work.

In imitation of the wise conductor, I will not try to draw conclusions about the work, expatiate on its pleasures and mysteries, or direct your interpretation of it. I will only tell two stories, one about what prompted the book, and the other about the process that created it.

•

Imagine a child raised not by wolves but by a cavil of philosophers. Call the child Perdita. When she comes of age, Perdita undertakes a journey through the wilderness, finding shelter along the way first with a kickback of politicians and later with a fantasy of cosmologists. After many trials and hardships, she happens on a vanity of poets, with whom she lives for a time. She falls in love, of course, with one or two, and adapts readily to her new community, smitten as she is with its language and at ease with its customs, which resemble those of the philosophers by whom she was raised.

Citizens of both tribes, as it happens, scribble messages on leaves and distribute them to others in their clan. However, Perdita finds some aspects of the poets' message-scribbling puzzling. The philosophers expect their fellows to disagree with what they write, scribbling alternatives and rebuttals on their own leaves and passing them around. They *want* such disagreement, consider it edifying, and feel disappointed, even disrespected, if their leaves prompt no counterleaves. Like the philosophers, the politicians and cosmologists revel in debate and rely on disagreement. The poets, though, expect their fellows to scratch new leaves with paeans of praise to them; they resent and find hurtful any other reaction. The response Perdita's youthful preceptors insisted was a sign of respect counts in her new community as the deepest of insults. Either praise or silence on a second leaf, upon threat of exile: such is the law Perdita learns from the poets.

Just as curious, from Perdita's point of view, is the penchant poets have for closed dialogues. Those who prefer oak leaves expect only other oak-leaf lovers to read their messages and they themselves rarely read messages on other leaves than oak, preferring in their long walks through the wilderness to pass by messages left on maple and birch. Because they *read* mostly messages on oak leaves, they also *respond* almost exclusively to messages on oak leaves.

Not content to accept passively the law of praise or silence, Perdita might scribble arguments against it on leaves of her own. But she might also try to resist that law in other ways: she might, for example, gather around her dissidents enough to question the customs, to see what more contentious counterleaves might look like in her new home. And rather than accepting closed dialogues, she might create schemes to get oak-leaf poets and birch-leaf poets writing to each other.

Having understood the parable, you, astute reader, will have inferred—correctly—that this book originated from a discontent over the dialogue in our world about poetry, similar in some ways to the discontent Perdita feels about the dialogue in hers, and from the sense, shared with Perdita, that solving the problems will less likely result from asserting another argument than from reinventing the conditions of the dialogue.

Those preexisting conditions of dialogue include reluctance to *argue* over poetry. We argue over votes in the Senate; over movies; over religious doctrines. Why do we soft-shoe around poetry? In part, I think, from the widespread but mistaken view that poetry is essentially emotional, combined with the (also mistaken) view that all emotions are equally valid and that therefore emotion cannot be the object of debate and evaluation. Certainly poetry appeals importantly to the emotions, but it does so as part of its appeal to the whole person (the body, the reason, the memory, and so on), not to the exclusion of other appeals. As for emotions, they vary in relevance, correspondence with reality, and other characteristics, leaving them, like ideas, subject to debate and evaluation. What Hilary Putnam says of temperament is true of emotion: it "is subject to criticism. Part of what philosophical conflict is about is determining what sort of [emotion] is best suited to the universe we live in." Among its other effects, timidity about conflict over poetry impairs the ability to determine what sort of emotion is best suited to one's world.

The poets in this book try, in their poems and in their responses to the poems of others, to determine what sort of emotion is best suited to the universe we live in. The poems talk of "forever waking" and being "excruciatingly awake"; they talk about "mak[ing] of struggle / an arrow" and "griev[ing] / The sinister loss." The responses engage those determinations. "I don't like my empathy solicited," says one respondent. "Experience presented is one thing, but being directed toward how to feel about it, well, I'd rather take a walk." Another observes that the tendency toward evaluation in the responses "seems to try to draw the work to some understood or implicit norm of coherence," an unsuitable pattern because "not everything needs to go to the middle way."

As it contests the premise that poetry is ultimately emotional, so this book questions the assumption that poetry is always primarily a vehicle of self-expression. Were that true, there would be reason for the law of praise or silence, since criticism of the poem would be immediate criticism of the poet. If the poem's content totalled to "I am such-and-such," then of course a negative evaluation of the poem would be an insult to the poet. Criticism would serve as a scarlet letter: a public ritual to enforce subjection of the individual to popular values. But if poetry is about the whole world, not only about oneself—if, in other words, it is public rather than private—then criticism need not be (and ought not be) ad hominem: it can be a debate about values rather than an enforcing of them. The conversation between poem and respondent can go in both directions: through the scarlet letter her community criticizes Hester, but so does she stand, whether they themselves recognize it or not, as a (brutal) critique of her community. In this book, the respondents might at first appear to have the final say, but if the responses interrogate the poems, so do the poems interrogate the responses.

•

Like Perdita, I created a scheme to encourage the conversation I wanted to hear: I invited a number of poets to send a short poem of their own choosing and to respond—blind and anonymously—to six or eight poems by other participants. I began inviting poets in early February of 2003—soon after Etruscan Press courageously committed to a project that risked flagrant failure—and continued into late April. During that time I invited eighty poets to participate, giving or sending each a description of the project. Eleven politely declined; many did not respond at all; some said they would participate but never sent a poem; and the thirty-three poets whose poems follow agreed to participate and did so. I aimed at convening a group that was diverse in its aesthetic no less than in its ethnic and gender composition. The thirty-three poets include women and men; poets of Asian, Hispanic, and African heritage; gay poets and straight; poets of widely varied styles and sensibilities; established poets and newer poets; poets from Boston to Honolulu, Wyoming to Florida.

I circulated the poems among the participants, "shuffling the deck" each time: poem A to poet B, poem B to poet C, and so on.

The recipient did not know the identity of the poet to whose poem he or she was responding. Participants understood that the poems would be published under the poet's name but that responses would remain anonymous. Each poet knows, therefore, that the responses to her or his poem came from other poets included in the anthology but not from which particular poets. For example, David Mason knows that all the responses to his poem were from other participants, but he does not know whether Carol Moldaw was or was not one of those who responded to his poem nor, if she was, which response was hers. The participants did not know the identity of the other participants until the book's publication nor did they see the responses to their own poems prior to publication.

I distributed the poems semi-randomly. About twice a week, I took whatever poems had been returned with responses, shuffled them, and sent them back out to the poets who had responded. I imposed a few constraints: of course I made sure that no poet responded more than once to the same poem, but I also tried to balance the gender of the respondents (to have roughly the same number of male respondents as female to any given poem) and I made sure that no poem went to the poet's spouse (the participants included two wife-husband pairs) or to someone I knew to be a close friend or immediate colleague of the poet (two of the poets teach in the same department; at least two of the participants I know to have been students of another; and so on). The one oversight I am aware of having made in that regard (sending a poem from one poet to another I knew, but had simply forgotten, was his good friend) was corrected by the recipient, who, recognizing the poem, sent it back without response and asked for another. No doubt there are alliances of which I am not aware, since I have not met all the poets who participated.

The scheme has inherent limitations, some of which the participants themselves have pointed out as part of their responses. It will not perfect the dialogue about contemporary poetry and put Perdita wholly at peace, but it does fulfill its aim of getting poets talking about each other's work across the usual patterns of conversation. It records a series of encounters between different premises about poetry, asking what happens when a poet who considers form the definitive aspect of poetry—and by form means iambic pentameter and rhyme—reads a poem written by a poet who thinks a poem's political implications matter more than its form and anyway by form means the visual appearance of a poem on the page; how a poet who considers it important to violate poetic tradition reads and evaluates a poem that attempts to adhere very strictly to a tradition; and so on. The anonymity of the dialogue ensured that its participants, at least for the sake of this project, concurred with the point of view formulated succinctly by the artist Michel Tapié: "Our interest is not in movements, but in something much rarer, authentic Individuals."

At one point in the dialogue, a participant asks: "[D]oes the fact that we make these comments anonymously encourage . . . greater frankness and objectivity or simply less responsibility for our opinions?" Fortunately for all of us who are able to overhear this conversation, its discussants chose the former route. I leave you now to the resulting pleasure and provocation.

WILD and Whirling WORDS

Carol Frost

GULL

Every wing, every instant burgeoning with wind

has an attendant grace. The sky sweats, copper

haze blears the horizon for tomorrow's storm

the gulls annunciate. Ah (you say), also consider

the flesh of the turtle burnt black by strange

decay—turnips gone bad crowding the air—

and the hoarse whispers of the sea,

Icarus consumed in the burning sea. Wild

honey drowned, nymphs, empty cans, plastic

flip-flops, boats broken from their moorings,

capsized, all are pulled down. Who rises?

Gulls steel their wings, their cries hardly

angelic, bruiting changes in weather,

but I have seen them make of struggle

an arrow, a silken figure, and a plumb bob,

whatever was needed while the winds clocked,

as if *if* they were miraculously related

to time, the storm would blow itself out.

Natural enough, that, but no less

beautiful, stopping in flight, racing, their breasts

now pink, now yellow in fallen sunlight.

•

I have to admit up front my prejudice toward most nature poetry. Nature is in such peril that unless a nature poem is saying "save nature for god sakes!" I often find the work too quaint for my tastes. Many contemporary nature poems seem to me to lack urgency or hit too many false notes, because so many people/poets are alienated from nature. But "Gull" really grabbed me when the "turnips gone bad" showed up. I really like the way Icarus and "plastic flip-flops" commingle in this poem, and the specificity of the "plumb bob" is amazing. I'm taken by the ending of the poem, especially the lines "Natural enough, that, but no less / beautiful . . . ," which questions the premise that all of us think that nature is beautiful. The logic here seems to imply that these gulls are beautiful even though they are natural, unenhanced. And for that reason I find "Gull" to be a satisfying and lovely poem, one that moves far beyond its apparent subject matter.

•

This poem works best when its lyricism is unfettered, as in the list of things, the "wild / honey drowned, nymphs, empty cans, plastic / flip-flops, boats broken from their moorings," pulled into the sea. There is something appealing in having nymphs (and Icarus) matter-of-factly next to empty cans and plastic flip-flops: it brings the mythical right into our debris-filled world, it saves the poem from preciousness while letting the dreamy in. The same is true of the description of the gulls making "of struggle / an arrow, a silken figure, and a plumb bob"—the accuracy and the lack of pretention in the image of the plumb bob balances the vaguer more elevated silken figure. The decision to justify the lines on the right instead of left works: it gives a physical sense of the gulls going against the wind. I'm less taken by the poem's rhetorical voice: "Ah (you say)," "who rises?" and the "that" in "natural enough, that" all feel like setups, otherwise gratuitous and a bit ingratiating. Though not in favor of quaintness, I have no prejudice against nature poetry per se. When this poem works, it is a matter of its grace—a grace that lets the sky sweat, that risks the complexity and momentary confusion of "as if *if*," and that doesn't make too much of its own loveliness while not forgoing it.

•

Since gulls by nature are scavengers, their juxtaposition with trash is hardly innovative. While this poem has its felicities (the turtle burnt black, turnips gone bad crowding the air, bruiting changes, the winds clocked), the poet's sense of what makes a poem is rather elementary in its use of:

1. poetic rhetoric: consider the flesh [Bible]; but I have seen them make [Eliot]
2. poetic nouns: wing, wind, storm, struggle
3. poetic modifiers: angelic, miraculously, beautiful
4. poetic verbs: fallen, consumed, drowned, capsized, pulled down
5. poetic abstractions: attendant grace, strange decay, burning sea, wild honey
6. poetic cliché: the storm would blow itself out
7. poetic gimmicks:
   —appropriating myth: Icarus, nymphs
   —cataloging images: empty cans, plastic flip-flops, boats broken, an arrow, a plumb bob
   —playing with form: right-justification

Indeed, the ingredients used in this poetic recipe can only make for a sickly sweet confection that is meant to taste like poesy. Nothing wrong with it per se—I just can't stomach it.

•

There are several aspects of this poem that excite me a great deal, and one or two aspects of it that interfere with my excitement. What I like best is the delicate, painterly, descriptive manner. Lines such as "The sky sweats, copper / haze blears the horizon for tomorrow's storm" fill the visual imagination. The tonal and imagistic complexities of the list of objects beginning "Wild / honey drowned" are rich, resonant. The "eye" that informs this poem is used to looking closely at art—and at life. "The hoarse whispers of the sea, / Icarus consumed in the burning sea" brilliantly suggests a ghost image of terrifying orality. Within its dominant tonal medium of "artificiality," the diction is as precise and flamboyant as it could possibly be.

But, finally, the artificiality of the diction does have consequences, at least for this reader. The "elegance" of words such as "angelic" and "bruiting" says, to that part of the ear listening to connotations more than to denotations, "This is gorgeous, what we're seeing." This implies that the emotional response predated the engagement with the objects of the poem, compared, for instance, to the drama of discovery depicted by the emergence, at the end of Elizabeth Bishop's "At the Fishhouses," of shockingly elevated, abstract diction from the flat diction of "direct observation." One feels there that Bishop's imagination did not want to be sentimental, but the beautiful pressure of reality forced it to be potentially sentimental. The "editorializing" tonal effect of "Ah" places this poem in the landscape of personality, "vision," rather than in the landscape of sight.

•

I want to read the white spaces of this poem as significant silences. Are the lines double-spaced or even triple-spaced? I believe the form of a poem has to be earned. If a poem has all of the lines justified on the right margin, there needs to be a point of resistance that the poem keeps confronting. The danger is for the form to be clever or contrived, but this poem struggles to attain a moment of stability in the context of a larger instability. The black lines exert pressure against, or are certainly in tension with, the white spaces, and so I believe the poem earns its form here.

I think there's a religious subtext that hasn't yet been discussed: consider the words "annunciate," "grace," "angelic," "fallen sunlight." At the end, the sunlight could be "fallen" because it's the end of the day, but "fallen" can also refer to the current condition of man. Without redemption, we look at gulls and find the way to make out of the coming, contentious storm "an arrow" or "plumb bob." (Does Hopkins hover in the background?) For this reader, the poem pivots at the strategic center with "Who rises?"

I too admire the "turtle burnt black," the "turnips gone bad," but I too am uneasy about the reliance on stating "miraculously" or "beautiful," when there might be a way to make it the thing itself. Yet the poem ends with a fine image and rhyme. Because "flight" is tucked inside the next-to-last line, the rhyme with "sunlight" gives the poem an unexpected moment of elegance and stability within the larger motion. And the shifting colors on the breasts of the gulls are rich and resonant.

•

I find this poem graceful and engaging, with many memorable lines. (I love "an arrow, a silken figure, and a plumb bob.") "Gull" seems to belong to the venerable tradition of bird poems in English (on skylarks, thrushes, nightingales, oven birds, etc.) that address poetry as well as nature—flight and song—but it does so by employing the deliberately unpoetic "gull." (Though the deliberately poetic also makes its appearance, in the surprising inclusion of "honey" and "nymphs." Maybe I am missing a reference in "Wild / honey drowned"?) By the way, is there supposed to be a comma after line 3? Otherwise I have trouble parsing the syntax.

I like how this poem proceeds by antitheses—by what sinks versus what rises. Another commentator has protested at the "gimmick" of appropriating myth, but I think Icarus is a risk that pays off here. Icarus, though winged, actually belongs to what sinks and is pulled down, and it is an interesting twist that the sea is referred to as "burning" (rather than the melting rays of the sun that it reflects). Time is also winged and makes its appearance in "every instant" and the "winds clocked." Gulls, being winged, might be associated with angels but their cries are "hardly" angelic (the line break also brings out the hardness in "hardly"). I was of two minds about "bruiting" at first. The word has strong overtones of Ransom to me. But I've decided I like it here—a pun on "bruting" or making animal and incarnate the changes of the weather.

William Heyen

ANDES FLAME

Other sacrificed maidens are found, chipped
from graves in the sacred mountains,
but this one won't be accessioned,
thawed, disrobed . . . a few threads

at a time. I see her in position, frozen,
my pottery set around her—black & red,
zigzag designs. I chose her, revered her,
died within prayer when I lost her,

but now we are almost translation
in that distance where heat from dead stars
still seeks her beneath my breastbone,
but cannot reach her, ever, love of mine. . . .

•

I'm struck first by what this lyric does not reveal. Structured as
what Helen Vendler terms a "then/now" poem, it offers neither
an antecedent context (we can't tell what's immediately
prompted the speaker's utterance or who the speaker is) nor
any specific narrative bridge between the "then" of the poem ("I
chose her, revered her, / died within prayer when I lost her")
and the "now" of the poem ("but now we are almost transla-
tion"). Though the poem's title and allusions to Incan ritual and

archaeological digs imply certain possibilities, these are various and increasingly seem, as the poem progresses, metaphorical and even mysterious. Is this because the poem is part of a larger, related group of poems that answer these questions? Is it because the answers to these questions are immaterial to the poem's intentions? Most important, do these unanswered questions detract from the experience of the poem? For this reader, the answer to that last question is no; while additional context might add to or alter somewhat the experience of emotions and ideas enacted here, the poem remains compelling without them. I am drawn to its rhythms—both in terms of its language (the poet's use of diction, syntax, the line, etc.) and in terms of its content, which, through metaphor and the speaker's recollections and declarations, moves from almost matter-of-fact statement to an increasing intensity of emotion that climaxes in the resonant and lovely trope of the final lines.

•

Like "She Dwelt among the Untrodden Ways" (1799) by William Wordsworth, this poem chooses to reveal almost nothing about the relationship between narrator and beloved, becoming oddly affective in its choice. The mild pun of the title, the possibility that the narrator may have been the beloved's murderer—the priest who sacrificed her—or one who witnessed her sacrifice, the fact that this maiden exists now, at the narrator's insistence, less palpably as mummified corpse than as "translation / . . . beneath my breastbone," all lend themselves to the unrestrained yet earned emotion of the final line. Such borderline sentimentality acknowledges risk, yet the poem remains true to its intentions. The precise visual details (the "few threads" and the pottery with its "black & red, / zigzag designs") have grounded the poem, allowing eyesight to deepen, finally, into vision ("that distance where heat from dead stars / still seeks her"). Wordsworth's Lucy (also "A Maid . . . / Half hidden from the eye") has been transported from "her grave" in the English

Lake District to one of the "graves in the sacred [Andean] mountains," each narrator sounding "oh" or "ever" against such inexpressible loss.

•

The imagined maiden is safe from becoming public, of belonging to others, of being "accessioned" like another sacrificed museum piece. The imagined maiden is the object—of desire, of attention, of language—secure under the breastbone, where the heart lies, where old flames burn.

•

With its ellipses, "Andes Flame" seems a fragment of a poem, perhaps a translation from a shard. Yet within the poem there are no fragments. The pottery is whole. The "maiden" herself is frozen, as the anachronistic terms "maiden," "revered," "breastbone," and "love of mine" might suggest, in a context as frozen as she is. Even her clothing is whole and resists breaking down into threads. Perhaps the secret to this twist of affairs is the fact that the speaker has "chosen" her, "covered" her, "died within prayer." Has the speaker preserved her wholeness at the speaker's own expense? The speaker's voice, the speaker's poem, is a sorry fragment, not fully translation but "almost translation," reached only by the futile heat of dead stars. It is no longer possible to write a fully Romantic poem of longing for an unattainable woman who embodies, conveniently, perfection. This poem does the best it can and, in falling short, reveals the ragged sadness of the attempt.

•

Had I not known that a living poet had written "Andes Flame," if I were on *Jeopardy!*, let's say, and Alex Trebek read me the opening stanza, I would have guessed something like: "Who is

Wordsworth?" I think the poem does what it sets out to do very well. I am particularly drawn to the fragmented quality, especially the first line's ending on "chipped." In that space between the first and second lines, the maidens are momentarily chipped, archaeological ruins themselves.

•

The eternal (and eternally lamenting) lover who pines for this (rather than any other) sacrificed maiden presents himself at once as the eternal or timeless lyric lover, the "I" of love poems generally ("love of mine"); as a sort of museum curator or archaeologist, using decidedly modern terms ("zigzag"; "accessioned," taken into a museum's collection), and as an Inca craftsman ("my pottery") who made the objects entombed with the maiden (and who may or may not have contributed more directly to her ritual death). The maiden is his "flame," in the modern colloquial sense of "old flame"; and being not just a dead young woman but the entombed victim of a ritual sacrifice, she endures beyond time, as the speaker perhaps will not (hence the comparison to Wordsworth's "Lucy" poems, which other readers bring up). I'm not sure, however, that the poem's diction really puts its historical analogies to enough use: the ancient, the modern, and the apparently timeless merge thematically, but the poem sounds decidedly modern throughout—I found myself wishing for more linguistic variety, for a more colorful palette of diction, one that devoted at least some time to archaisms or to something that sounded at least partly alien. (Compare the archaic/modern diction in some poems by John Peck, or some of Robert Duncan, or Lucie Brock-Broido's "Carrowmore.") One might defend the poem by arguing that its inability to reach linguistically beyond contemporary spoken standard English mirrors the speaker's inability to reach his beloved: Do we have, in fact, a modern archaeologist—at the Smithsonian, say—trying and failing to imagine himself as an Incan ceramicist, trying and failing to liken his lost love to a sacrificed maiden, since both are gone for good?

Diane Glancy

CAN YOU IMAGINE HEARING
NO STORIES?

1.
How do you begin a story?

You face the silence so dense the words are *magnetified* metal fillings, but you begin to pry.

You put both feet on the floor you sit in a chair you open your mouth. You speak to the story as if it were already there. You remember a stray cat who came around and you left the door ajar and you see him while you're at your desk from the corner of your eye he walks past the door one way then another and soon he jumps on your desk scaring you both but he's there and you reach out once and once again and soon he lets you touch his head.

You say, *ho* nothing, *hey*, my Indian grandmother couldn't speak, didn't speak, my mother had no stories, wouldn't, because maybe she had none to tell except we lived
worked
sorrowed
died.

2.

No, you don't offer the story a corral or even the pasture.
You offer it the whole continent.

You hear a buzz, a hum, which is the clump that forms
before a word.

You hear the word that comes from the hum.
Then others follow.
They stand together, shivering.

You separate the words from one another.
They won't want to at first though some come forward
to stand next to other words.
They learn to adapt, move over, and change in relation to
others.

That's how story is a process of learning how to trust
before you hear.

A phenomenon that nothing longs for something more than
something longs for nothing.

3.

Your words travel the air-space between others, and there
is a *hereness*, a connection, and soon your one voice is a
cropduster that turns into a Concord when you see it's a
matter of magnitude

say the prairie air-corridor at full amp.

•

What's the difference between narrative and story? What's the difference between stories told and untold? What's the difference between a story told once, a story told twice, and a story told many times? Does a story have to find its own way of telling itself or does the teller tell it? How can you tell the told from the tale?

Poetry is the art of listening. Even when you write in silence, by yourself, you're listening to the way the words will be heard, responding to that hearing. Oh well, poetry isn't anything, that's just my idea of poetry, my story today (I have other versions).

I can no more imagine hearing no stories than I can imagine telling no stories. To imagine is to do both those things.

"You hear the word that comes from the hum." The huhuman.

"That's how story is a process of learning how to trust before you hear." You don't hear anything unless you first listen, just as you can't have truth without trust or thirst without memory.

Longing for nothing is often the only way to get anywhere.

Or so the story goes.

•

I am most interested in this poem when it most closely approaches the inarticulate. The word "magnetified," followed as it is by the verb "pry" suggests to me the way the story is caught in one's mouth like fillings or teeth, that it must be pried open and extracted. When the language switches to the cat, though the metaphor is different, I also find it interesting, for the language moves differently as if with the cat. I do wonder, given the rhetorical question of the title, what the poem is trying to say: Is it about the difficulty of telling the story that one wants to tell? Or is it about the inescapability of the story? That no matter where we begin, in the mouth, with the cat, in the groupings of words, in the flight of a jet, we find ourselves spinning a narrative? In the first response, there are phrases:

"Poetry is the art of listening. Even when you write in silence, by yourself, you're listening to the way the words will be heard, responding to that hearing. Oh well, poetry isn't anything, that's just my idea of poetry, my story today (I have other versions).

I can no more imagine hearing no stories than I can imagine telling no stories. To imagine is to do both those things."

that seem to me to be rather simplistic, prosaic statements of intent, and they seem to be at odds with the more complex nexus of meaning that the poem creates in the cat, in the magnetified mouth, in the prairie corridor at full amp.

•

While praising story, "Can you imagine" playfully eludes and exposes narrative conventions. This hybrid piece doesn't begin, "Once upon a time," "Sing, Heavenly Muse," "Call me Ishmael," or "A priest, a minister, and a rabbi walked into a bar"—gambits storytellers use to guide and shape our listening. Instead, it resists a single pattern by alluding to many, "travel[ing] the air-space between" pattern and chaos, between the temporal movement of plot and the frisson between syllables like "dense" and "silence"; "ho" and "hey"; "cropduster" and "Concord." In this infinite fraction the listener attends to those aspects too large (continents), too disparate (buzz/clump) or too ephemeral (the prairie air-corridor) to yield to narrative treatment. It is not our disbelief in story but our belief in story's closure that is suspended as we glimpse (thrilled, terrified) a void we are teased into imagining.

•

The axis of absence and presence haunts and animates this poem. "You face the silence so dense the words are magnetified." Is magnetified a portmanteau derived from "magnetized" and "calcified"? I don't know. I believe a poem does not need to mirror life but can enact its own discoveries. This poem, with its keen attunement to silence and sound, its intense focus on language and the process of creation, does so: "story is a process of learning how to trust before you hear."

As I reread this poem, I wonder if there are too many "you"s in the first section. Is it deliberately jarring, haunting, or carping to do so? I also wonder if, in the second section, "They learn to adapt, move over, and change in relation to others" is insufficiently calibrated to the situation at hand. (In contrast, "They stand together, shivering" has a frisson.) These quibbles aside, I like how the "stray cat" is conjured by memory, and how the initial fright settles into familiarity. In the third section, the shift from "cropduster" to "Concord" is riveting, and I agree with the previous, cogent response: "It is not our disbelief in story but our belief in story's closure that is suspended."

•

Magnetified metal fillings? What would these be? In your teeth? Fillings, not filings, which would make some sense? So your teeth are clamped shut by words? Or do the magnetified poles drive your mouth permanently open? No, you open your mouth in the next paragraph, so it must have been shut. . . .

In other words, this poem begins with such an incompetent metaphor that it never really recovers. It gets better, though. The cat. The politics of Indian blood—a relationship between storytelling and land acquisition. Storytelling and adaptation "in relation to others."

Still, this poem's pseudo-philosophical diction leaves me cold. I have to decide to "appreciate" an unfinished piece of writing, and at this moment I am unwilling to do so. I think this poem needs to go back to the drawing board.

•

I am totally drawn into this poem. For me, it's about silencing, being silenced, silencing ourselves. I kept waiting for the revelation, the "story" that could not previously be told but that would now, in this poem, be told. But that story never came. Instead of experiencing disappointment, I was haunted. The poem's three parts, three attempts (it seems to me) to get at a narrative, delightfully fail. "You hear a buzz, a hum, which is the clump that forms before a word." This poem is like an engine trying to turn over, a tooth hanging by that last thread of gum. It is about the anticipation of story.

Bruce Bond

TO THE SKYWALKERS

Looking up I always weaken
in the knees, to see them walk
the headless skeleton they're in,

these men who weather a craze
of breezes, stepping from scaffolding
to beam and back, flagging the giant

girders down and starring them
with rivets; with every steel seam
they weld, a fainting spell of sparks.

I've always wondered what it took
to feel a god over your shoulder,
there where the blue flame sizzles and bites,

to know the opening beneath you
has you like a hunger: you listen
in vain for the hammer as it falls.

Doubtless they must feel sheltered
in their skins, quiet as a high
room cradled in the sound of rain.

The higher they are the slower
the dark particles of strangers
gathered and swept from curb to curb.

A lesser man would dissolve
in the Pacific of what he sees.
Somewhere the intricate gem

of a taxi flashes as it corners.
Not that life is any cheaper
where they work. Anything but.

Only that they feel closer, not
merely to the virginal sky,
but to their bodies, like an exile

alone with his mother tongue,
turning to himself and singing.
It seems so deft, more cunning

than words this faith, and older,
this gift of nerve that holds them
to their task: each eye is a child's

crystal clinging to its bright string.
It wakes them to the world they watch,
time and again, forever waking,

until, that is, they descend
as the sun descends into their lives,
into night that falls between them

where they lie, face up on their pillows,
a black shaft above and below
to guide their every step of the way.

•

There's a kind of poem that demands much of a theoretical mind for its justification as well as its understanding. Then there's the kind that relies foremost on physical accuracy, a fundamental aspect of good writing in most traditions. "To the Skywalkers" is the latter, its ideas sublimated to its well-wrought images.

First, this strong sense of vertigo, the terrifying height of workers who spend their days between heaven and earth—a serious extension of those ladders and birches in Frost poems. And this poem is full of evocation—phrases like that "fainting spell of sparks" that capture the particulars of work—something for which I have great sympathy.

In the fourth tercet the poem makes plain its metaphysical interests, alluding to the hammer-wielding Norse god, Thor. By stanza 10, with its "virginal sky," there's the Christian implication. None of these is dogmatic, of course. They're playfully metaphysical, like the supreme fiction in Stevens. And by the poem's conclusion we're imaging those workers at home in their beds, the ominous "black shaft above and below." This is suggestive of one's suspension in sleep, of shaft graves, and so on. But more important, it captures that vertiginous sense you have if you've spent your day high up—a sense I remember from rock-climbing days.

The poem commits one contemporary sin, implying that all such workers are male. But we're grown-ups and can read beyond the obvious. It is very fine work.

•

This is a narrative poem about walking the scaffolding of a building-in-progress. The "I" brings in the poem, then disappears after the fourth stanza. After that, various images are at work: the sizzle of a blue flame, a "cradled" room, a flashing taxi. Men walk in a magical world as if children, until they come back to the world's ground level. The poem ends with their sleep and a question that opens the possibilities of meaning. What is the "black shaft above and below?" The girders of the building? Their bodies? The nights they lie between? In the end, the poem becomes as unsettling as slipping over the edge of a dream. Then the poem is the "I" facing the ominous portent of the shaft in a dream that walks the inverted, insular life on the high wire of a building that has not yet come into being.

•

The method of this poem is traditionally New Critical: a single image is developed until it becomes a symbol. I find that I like my reader's faith that acute, accurate, emotionally charged perception predates the composition of the poem. The imagery always reveals both the literal and the figurative simultaneously; I much admire lines such as: "The higher they are the slower / the dark particles of strangers / gathered and swept from curb to curb." On the rare occasions when in my writing I am able to make contact imaginatively with the outer world, as has happened here, I have the thrilled feeling that I've written something beyond what Coleridge, I think, labeled "fancy." This poem is making that contact throughout itself beautifully. The purely verbal gestures that have the faint clang of cliché ("their every step of the way," "Anything but," etc.) do not bother me— as in Elizabeth Bishop's poetry, the integrity of this voice is in its accuracy, not its "wit." Good work!

•

I take the "black shaft above and below" in this final poem's final tercet to mean both the literal and the metaphorical girder we all walk between safety and disaster, faith and fear (and fearlessness). What most intrigues me about this poem is its clearly wrought imagery that succeeds in being both visually accurate and intellectually slippery at the same time. The poem moves quickly from personal musing to physical description to spiritual meditation to comparison, creating a kind of "falling" effect for me that very nicely echoes one of the poem's subjects. Reading this poem after a semester of studying mostly L=A=N=G=U=A=G=E poets and New York School–style poets (and a whole slew of first books that fall somewhere in-between these schools) as well as mourning the death of a mentor and a divorce, I'm shocked by the hot relief that washed through me at the sight of these tercets. I suppose it is because this is the kind of poem I was trained best to read in school, but its well-wrought language that allows for chaos as well as formal control speaks forcefully to the current evolutions in my own aesthetic and personal life. "To the Skywalkers" became my own momentary girder, and though this doesn't say anything of use to the poet (or to the reader wanting to understand poetry), right now I'm deeply grateful for the work.

•

Tightrope-walking, high-wire acts, and trapeze-swinging have often been contorted into tropes for the art of poetry, and it speaks to the cunning and authenticity of this poem that such a reading occurs to me only long after the first line of "To the Skywalkers" weakened my knees, propelling me back into a childhood of word- and work-play, of magical association and ever-shifting dimensions. I'm not sure exactly what qualities dissolved my critical sensibilities nor if this dissolution made me "a lesser" reader, but I am sure that no poem can really move me until a few cables are cut and I step into the air beyond the scaffolding of my expectations. I would not abandon myself altogether—"Anything but." I continue to review the poem's intricate workings: the daring associations—"virginal," "string," "nerve," "faith," "Pacific," "crystal," that lean almost too far into space before being pulled back by the sound-net, by stanza and syllabics. I regain my balance not to access nor to instruct, but to savor, in another mode, my wonder, "like an exile alone with his mother tongue."

•

Although the poem begins with the speaker's physical response, a feeling of weakness, it immediately lifts us into the near-sky, where we remain—looking down—experiencing the graceful precariousness of the construction workers. This poem achieves its sinewyness through deft enjambment and diction (as in "flagging the giant / / girders down and starring them / with rivets" and "the opening beneath you / has you like a hunger: you listen / in vain for the hammer as it falls." The poem suspends us surely; very quickly we feel confident it won't drop us. I delight in jumping line to line, stanza to stanza, feeling a confidence akin to what the workers must feel as they step from girder to girder, their tool belts shifting, the danger balanced by the thrill. At a couple places I feel myself flailing to right myself ("the virginal (?) sky" line 29 and "It [string? crystal? eye? task?] wakes them to the world . . ." line 38), but at the end I am carried off safely.

Cate Marvin

INSIDE THE TREMBLING RESTAURANT

It was not I who sought the young fool.
It was the young fool who sought me.
Fell me to rooms till I was fisted by shadow.
Fell to me like lamplight, skin soft as ermine.
Bought my drinks till I drank his pockets dry.

A sweetness equal to hibiscus, his mouth
bordered on illegal—my coat crawled off
my shoulders, lay pooled and patient below
the bar stool. I heard rain slapping windows,
darkness losing itself to gutters, waitresses

clearing glasses, the ocean from a thousand
miles away, my mouth knowing him as it
loves water. Scarves of air moved above
us, as the ceiling's fan swung low above
us, and the young women hid themselves

against the wallpaper's ancient flowers,
unafraid, wishing to claim him in a glance.
That century the nights lapped around us,
birth dates departed, and the constellations
spun swift and acrobatic. By then I had

forgotten to teach him a new vocabulary.
What he will not understand: *I cannot eat.*
I am still a child. And when I try to fit my
tongue around the word *love*, dogs whine
at my door, and rats shiver in their gutters.

•

The deliberate estrangements of this poem leave me with mixed feelings, alternately intrigued and irritated. On the one hand, I'm reminded of a lot of early Modernist poetry and perhaps some painting as well. The poet seems to be straining a bit for effect, so I strain to meet the poet and wonder if it's made worth my effort.

How should I respond to the use of "Fell" in the third line? It's not a present imperative, since the line is in the past tense. Does "fisted" refer to being beaten or being "fist-fucked"? Is there a difference?

A kind of desperate sensuality takes over in the poem, and one gets a sense of a feeding frenzy of a relationship. Nevertheless, this poem only manages to make me glad I don't know the speaker personally.

And those rats in the gutters—pure Eliot—what are we to make of them? Trying to be new, this poet accomplishes something rather old.

•

I too am very perplexed by the use of "fell" in line 3. I'm rather perplexed, actually, by the whole first stanza, which seems too archaic in tone to fit the rest of the poem. Is this speaker a child molester? My first thought went to Ai's poem "Child Beater," whose title clearly sets up a persona for the reader. This poem doesn't quite offer its readers that distance—which is what, I think, the tone is trying to do. The first two lines seem like a complete rationalization for the rest of the poem, the kind of thing we hear all the time from wife-beaters (she hit me first) and pedophiles (the child came on to me). I do admire this poem for its risky subject matter, but this reader, at least, would have liked a few more hints as to what was literally going on.

•

The poem reminds me that seduction poems are often celebrations of the speaker/seducer's rhetorical prowess as much as they are blazons to the beloved's beauty and other virtues; think of the nifty syllogism in "To His Coy Mistress." And "Inside the Trembling Restaurant" makes clear that its main interest is more the power of words than the power of sex. The poem's insistent rhetorical flowers (like the chiasmus of lines 1–2) bloom throughout the poem, leading us to the turn, at line 21, where the seduction seems to wilt because the speaker forgot "to teach him a new vocabulary": love isn't part of it.

•

The first two lines bear the stereotypical arch sound of an old queen, and there's the word "fisted" in the third line, but it is still not clear whether this poem is spoken by a man or woman. And it should be clear. . . . We have a sometimes vaguely tropical imagery here with hibiscus and scarves of air and ocean with nights that lapped, but what and where in dream or reality is the Trembling Restaurant? We should know. . . . And just what is it that necessitates these particular observations/reminiscences by our speaker? We ought to sense some coherence but can't really discover voice or character, or define the operative obsessions here. . . . The poem makes good reading once or twice, is intriguing, but it's finally uncomfortably diffuse, has been let go of by the poet prematurely. The poem gutters and goes out. . . .

•

The strength of this poem lies primarily in the evocative figurative energy of its parts, conjuring as they do a sadistic sensuality haunted by both intimacy and distance. In such a world, the urge to connect contains its own repression, the desire to devour, to deny, to possess—in short to remain a child. The flirtation with conventionally ominous imagery—rain, darkness, the night—is characteristically renovated by hallucinatory twists of metaphor—the rain "slapping windows," the darkness "losing itself to gutters," the nights that "lapped around us"—in each case a tonal instability, a sense of the world's loveliness and disgrace. Yes, the third and fourth lines stand out as the most confusing. And yes, the closure with the rats in the gutter offers the most derivative and familiar image in the poem. "Gutters" as the last word in the poem is particularly disappointing since it is not fresh to the poem rhetorically or conceptually. What is most interesting at the poem's end is the fact that the rats shiver in connection with the word "love," the fact that they embody a fear not simply of degrading hunger but also of an opening, of connection, of moving through that proverbial door. And what but a dog could figure so centrally as an archetype of *both* appetite and the need to love? What but a dog evokes so immediately a sense of the loyal and the derided, the devoted and the suppressed?

•

I love the title, and there is much in this poem to like, the visceral imagery and personification (the coat crawling off the shoulder, the scarves of air). Ultimately, though, I'd have to agree with the other comments here, that this doesn't quite come out from under the shadow of that Red Rock, Eliot. (Don't get me wrong, I love Eliot.)

I feel that the poem really begins in the second stanza; that's where I become interested ("A sweetness equal to hibiscus, his mouth" would be a great opening line)—and drops off some-where before or during the last stanza. The last line that really grips me is "against the wallpaper's ancient flowers." After that it seems to slide into Modernist-sentimental. (Prufrock can get away with the self-pity because of, among other things, the ironic distance inherent in his ridiculous name.) On the other hand, the voice does intrigue me, and I'd like to read more work by this poet.

Timothy Liu

HOMO EX HUMO

A dawn washed clean by sun inviting stain

Bedroom windows that shudder each time

A train rides past a wrist a plaster cast

So pendulous on winter roads that wind

Through woods unmasked by spring a page

Torn from a book of birds love sometimes

Flies shells washed up on a mountainside

Where copies of testaceous malacology

Vanish into biblical illustration color

Patterns that conceal or reveal taxonomy

As sooty prints scumble across offshore

Refineries discarded bones to avoid an eye

That follows finger holes labile puzzles

Probe a cranial angle where catechisms

Come apart at the seams from dust thou

Art and to dust thou burnt-hair smell

Of a spider's legs dangling over halogen

•

I always ask my students if they want the reader to say, "Hmmm, you've organized some language intelligently here" or "My goodness, this is fabulous—give me another!" For what it's worth, "Homo Ex Humo" can elicit only the first response. L=A=N=G=U=A=G=E poetry always demonstrates how smart the author is, and perhaps the reader should feel flattered to be addressed as an equal in terms of intelligence. But the whole proposition is self-defeating; you can argue aesthetics all day long, yet a university press editor who is locked unwillingly into a L=A=N=G=U=A=G=E poetry series complained to me recently that "the books don't get reviewed and nobody buys them." Most readers want to be engaged emotionally as well; the kindergartner grows up and gets smarter, true, but never loses that basic desire for pleasure. Author, beware: you can still write about "testaceous malacology," but do so pleasurably.

•

Pause in middle of Line

This poem is a bit of a "labile puzzle" itself, relying on caesuras and phrasing to signal its mid-thought shifts, and it succeeds when its precise language is matched by precision of usage, of vision; it falters, just past the middle, when it isn't. It draws the reader in with a cinematographic ease that offsets the conventionality of its initial images and then it plays with our poetic expectations and desires, sometimes fulfilling our desire for beauty in unexpected ways ("a page / Torn from a book of birds love sometimes / Flies"), sometimes abruptly confounding it, as when, with enjambment, the "offshore" that "sooty prints scumble across" turns into "offshore / Refineries." With its internal and half rhymes, its unbelabored pentameter base, its varied levels of diction, it has an idiosyncratic lyricism that affords many discrete moments of delight, some simple, such as "a wrist a plaster cast," some more complex, as in "a cranial angle where catechisms / Come apart at the seams." At times the poem stumbles over itself: "inviting stain," with its vague grammatical placement and vague symbolism, spoils the first line for me even as "sun" and "stain" resonate nicely. I don't so much dislike "testaceous malacology" as, again, think that the grammar of its phrasing makes it cloudier than it should be: malacology is a science—what does it mean that there are "copies" of it? And isn't testaceous malacology a bit redundant? What is it avoiding "an eye"? The prints? The phrase intrudes, breaks the trance. However, the poem rights itself, and the ending is lovely, the phrase we all know dropped midway to a precise and unexpected illustration of it, the "burnt-hair smell / Of a spider's legs dangling over halogen." I like the overall lyricism of this poem, even as it plays hide and seek.

It is ridiculous—unconscionable even—and a transparent ploy to judge a poem without examining it and then to use that judgment as a lead-in for a diatribe against a poetic school that, rightly or wrongly, the poem (the poet) is perceived as belonging to. Pity the first respondent's poor students.

•

The title is a Latin pun, meaning "man from the earth," attributed to the fourth-century Christian father Lactantius. The "mystic current of its meaning"—Poe's phrase—has something to do with the spiritual life, flowing from the image of absolution in the opening line through "biblical illustration" and "catechisms" to the concluding lines with their ancient injunction and their allusion to Jonathan Edwards's sermon, "Sinners in the Hands of an Angry God," delivered in 1741 during the Great Awakening ("The God that holds you over the pit of hell, much as one holds a spider or some loathsome insect over the fire, abhors you and is dreadfully provoked"). The poem seems to suggest that absolution requires sin ("inviting stain") as much as sin requires absolution, and that despite the natural tendency to unburden ourselves ("woods unmasked by spring"), guilt ("an eye / That follows") is what makes us human. The conflation of hell ("burnt-hair smell / Of a spider's legs dangling over") and heaven (the "halo" in "halogen," though the slant rhyme of "smell / hal . . ." also implies hell) in the final lines evokes the duality by which we live rather than the singularity ("from dust thou / Art and to dust thou") by which we die.

While I recognize the poem's intelligence, I remain wary of its somewhat arbitrary imagery and sloppy syntax. I dislike its lack of human warmth. It seems intent on its idea from the start, allowing itself no license. The philosopher John Dewey believed that artists "learn by their work as they proceed, to see and feel what had not been part of their original plan and purpose," but this poem seems written by fiat.

•

Yes, the title meaning "man from the earth" suggests that man rises out of corruption and sin, the "stain" that, given the slippery ("labile") syntax of the poem, could be what is invited by the sun or what invites the sun (more precisely the "sun-inviting stain") or even an appositive for "sun" which is restated as the "inviting stain." The lack of punctuation offers here a form of precision. In each case the sullied world is engaged with the charity of light, each world inviting and creating the possibility of its opposite. So too the image of the grace of dawn becomes echoed in that halo of the halogen to end the poem, an image of hell surely, of acrid ruination, but also of a particular kind of lamplight, a desk light, the illumination of study that would make a permanence, a taxonomy, of the dead and dying. The force of spring, of rebirth, and the love it engenders are registered in the word, the page, which would chase the birds, flying as they do (what finer tribute), becoming unstable in the process. One might be reminded here of Williams's "Spring and All." Yes, "testaceous malacology" is ugly and redundant but, one could argue, self-consciously so, since the words exemplify and embody the cognitive mind in its awkward, doomed attempt to know, to copy, to categorize, to arrest. (I'm not sure this is reason enough to subject us to the sudden clang of the language.) The phrase points to that which yields to faith and its colors. Here I find one of the most awkward lines of the poem ("vanish into biblical illustration color / patterns"); the figure is vague and rings false. It feels as though the ideas governing the poem have imposed themselves in the form of a metaphor that is too loosely hinged and blurry. In time even the categories of faith, the catechisms, "come apart" as the stuff of the earth caught up in the force of change. It's true; the poem even as it challenges the effectiveness of a stilted taxonomy asks us to engage in a rather cognitive enterprise in order to understand enough to enjoy the art. It's not what I would call a speedy poem, not quick to surprise us with its primary beauty, with its musical or emotive power. At times it feels as though this archer has put too many feathers on his or her arrow. But it is a highly layered, language-intensive, and inventive poem, and I continue to find much to admire in it.

•

Okay, *mea culpa*, I cheated. I glanced at the poem's Latin title, suffered a flashback to the Jesuits, and quickly scrolled down to crib from my fellow acolytes. What a dissonant choir! If nothing else, "Homo Ex Humo" has provided an occasion for brilliance. The only problem is, now I can't read the poem afresh. I don't know what my first reaction to "testaceous malacology" would be. Since I'm nobody, I can safely reveal that I had to look it up.

But I'm fine with that—poems ought to "include history" (though part of me pines for the days when the management of W&WW dispatched sonnets). But in this case, as respondents 2 and 4 point out, the phrase is "ugly and redundant," revealing not intelligence but pedantry.

Perhaps you cheated too, reader. Maybe not just on this poem. You can tell me, since you're nobody too (there's a pair of us, don't tell!). If your eyes have sometimes slid down a poem to luxuriate in a critique, then perhaps you feel, as I do, that cushioning poems in exegesis is a gift and a curse. It's wonderful to be pillowed, even on a page; I often feel lonely reading poems and I'm grateful for the company. I'm lured by the conversation—which seems in places more brilliant than the poems themselves. But it's hard work climbing back upstairs. For instance, left to myself I might have grasped for some meaning tantalizingly promised by "Homo Ex Humo" until I came to the penultimate lines, where I might have dismissed the poem as an exercise in poor punning. Who knows?

As it is, I'm intrigued that others find "much to admire" in this poem. And while I agree that it's foolish to use one poem to attack a movement (and if we judge poetry by sales, who shall escape whipping?), it's disingenuous to suggest that "Homo Ex Humo" be considered without access to the theories from which it emerges. Maybe I would have failed to appreciate "Homo Ex Humo" without guidance; but now I'm glad of its presence, because it hones my appreciation of possibilities, challenging me to associate without narrative, or logic, or emotion, led by chance, sound, and a glimpse of a kaleidoscopic world.

•

This poem has very even lines, generally between five and eight words. It seems to work by apocopation (seeming to offer the first part of a phrase or sentence only) and anacolouthon (shifting the grammatical construction in midstream), but it doesn't quite. The poem has been constructed somewhat (but not totally constructed) to make each line both intact on its own, readable in isolation, and enjambed, joined, readable only as linked. This effect of both singular lines and hinged lines is achieved curiously—by the space between each line, by the absolute lack of punctuation, and by the capital letter (formerly so conventional! now so rare!) at the beginning of each line. The double effect is also achieved by words such as *wind* and *cast* and *stain* that might be nouns or verbs, hence demanding that the reader shift grammatical structures. However, this fascinating instability is not pursued at the same rate and intensity throughout the poem; it resurfaces later only in the words "color" and "puzzles." And maybe "Flies." The prettiest part is probably "wind / Through woods unmasked by spring a page / Torn from a book of birds." And that is very pretty, indeed. Otherwise I am not sure what the point is (some point about how all things are joined in nature but these being ruptured by our man-the-master biblical tradition?). The nice swinging movement is interrupted by that lump of diction "testaceous malacology" (the shell-like study of mollusks?) which is a unique instance in this poem, not to speak of relatively unparsable. This phrase must be important enough to the poet to risk disturbing the otherwise fairly lyric surface and to risk receiving all the criticism about awkward inappropriateness that the phrase evokes, but so far I can't get any tread on a plausible reason why it is so important that those risks must be taken.

Susan Aizenberg

MEETING THE ANGEL

Not as a bird with twelve black wings and an eye
and a tongue for each of us. (Someone dies
each time he blinks.) And not shrouded in celestial
light, a fair-haired castrato. Not as Samael,
angel of poison, his venomous sword quivering
above the parched, open mouths of the dying.
He did not come as Azrael, *whom God helps,*
bearing apples so sweet their fragrance kills
our fear of leaving this known world. What did we
know of death, of suffering? Each day for weeks
we drove the autumn highway to the clinic,
where the angel's rough map ablated J.'s skin
with the blue tattoos of radiology, black
dissolve of surgical stitches. And like, or unlike
God, he was always with us, among the lush,
ongoing trees, the small mercies of fresh
air and afternoon light leavening the cracked
glass, our hearts' stutter, as we reached the exit.

•

This is a beautiful poem. I love its precision of image, form—the
quality of the writing on that technical level seems to have to do
with the quality of emotional and intellectual response to the

material. There is a great deal of beauty in the tension between the flamboyant, utterly appropriate depictions of the various possible imaginary angels and the prosaic realities of a clinic, radiology . . . the hospital landscape that is summoned so delicately into the reader's mind. I admire very much the skillful modulation away from description into abstraction in phrases such as "the lush, / ongoing trees, the small mercies of fresh / air and afternoon light leavening the cracked / glass. . . ." Ongoing, mercies, leavening: these words are so particular and so exact, both denotatively and connotatively, that they completely avoid the easy, breezy "rhetoricalness" often seen in writing that articulates the ways in which the world is perceived through the prism of self-awareness. Great poem!

•

To write about pain is always the great problem, isn't it. To write about one's own pain is fraught with danger of falling into the maudlin and the self-pitying. To write about the pain of others is an unconscionable arrogance—I personally have always hated the word "empathy," with its implication that one can feel what others feel. Well, we can't. We can try to sympathize, we can know our own pain and hope to understand that the pain of another must be something like but never exactly like that of the other.

To meet the pain of the other halfway is the great, even heroic ambition of this poem. Although one might question whether Rilke has marked out this territory for his own with such authority that we should enter it only tremblingly, nevertheless the image—concept, implication—of the angel is too useful to ignore, and in this case the angel does its work as a terrible, threatening, unknowable force, like disease itself: someone dies each time he blinks. Was it good or bad that "he" was always with us, the angel behind the bushes, "among the lush, / ongoing trees"? Who can say? I keep returning to the image of the apples "so sweet their fragrance kills / our fear of leaving this known world." That the word "kill" would appear in this phrase, this context of sensuous excess, and that killing would be associated with knowledge of the world—and associated with anesthesia, evoking Eve and Adam's forgetfulness, evoking Snow White's fall into a coma, and finally recalling the sweet smell of ether—all of this delicate associating is where the power of this poem rises.

•

More than the poem, or the bulk of the commentary it elicited, I was drawn to the previous respondent's antipathy to empathy. I suppose I could equally say the foundation of language is empathy, that empathy is what allows us to get the sense of something and that its absence puts us outside the possibilities for meaning. But I don't like my empathy solicited. Experience presented is one thing, but being directed toward how to feel about it, well, I'd rather take a walk. Problem is: Is it really possible for a poem not to tip its didactic hat? Poems can't just be; they always mean more than we might want to say or hear. Even the bracketing of experience leans toward a mode of experience.

The respondent praises the beauty of this poem and the exactness of its images. Maybe this is what I like least. The poem's polish makes a glossy surface in which I see myself staring, barred from making it to the other side. Angels are not just literary conceits or supernatural realities. The angelic might be a moment of grace in which the images we use to measure out, contain, or shield our suffering melt away. That would mean not using images to symbolize the real but rather letting the real pour in through the cracks between the words. To do that is as impossible as meeting an angel.

•

Watch my sentences, the stoic master Frost said. The first half of "Meeting the Angel" is rendered in six, its second half in two, and what we feel by way of this swelling, bottom-heavy closure is quiet astonishment that we can come into the presence of an angel so unexpectedly different from those of the four negations with which the poem begins.

The learned witness and his loved one—is this a pre-elegy, or has J. died for whom he now must speak?—were at first innocent. ("What did we / know of death, of suffering?) But their experience and now, here, memory compose. The two novitiates became acquainted (to echo Frost) with the angel of science (clinic and mapped radiology) and of autumn air— a fusion of technology and nature, stitches and trees, machine trees and growing trees—as they reached heart and highway denouement together. The fear of leaving the known world remains with them, the stutter. "Celestial light" was then, the commoner reality of "afternoon light" is now. All we can hope to feel, but which can be felt. This poem is not primarily about the angel but about *meeting* the angel of small mercies. But, yes, mercies.

•

I have to say: what a beautiful poem, with a crevice stitched right through it. I liked the words that flicked up other words beneath them: skills for kills (line 8), flesh for fresh (line 16), life leaving for light leavening (line 17). I liked the smooth and lush poem cracked with the ultraviolence of disease.

•

Empathy, like language itself, is necessarily an imperfect tool. And, like language, empathy is process. I have to trust in the possibilities of both empathy and communication, even as I know I will never fully reach a static understanding of what others mean and how they feel—because without that stab at the impossible, what would I be? And if a poet refuses to believe in the possibility of reaching toward correspondence with a subject or a reader, she will have sacrificed a dimension of her poems—not the only pleasure this reader seeks, but a principal one. I think, moreover, that it's an injustice to say this poem "solicits empathy." While it's closer to say that the speaker tries "to meet the pain of the other halfway," the poem's ending clearly depicts the impossibility of doing so. The angel with whom the speaker finally walks is an inescapable awareness of J.'s illness. But isn't this also the angel of survival, of gratefully and guiltily drinking in "the small mercies of fresh air and afternoon light?" In eighteen lines, the poet captures a complex of emotions—sorrow and relief, struggle and surrender—with considerable technical style.

David Kirby

YOUR MOMMA SAYS
OMNIA VINCIT AMOR

Running down the Via degli Annibaldi
I hear Aretha say
my momma said leave you alone
and as I hurry up the steps
of the church of San Pietro in Vincoli
I hear her say my daddy said come on home
and as I turn to go down the right aisle
she says my doctor said take it easy
and then I stop right in front
of Michelangelo's *Moses:*
oh but your loving is much too strong
for these chain chain chains
which were used to bind St. Peter in Palestine
and are themselves preserved under glass
in the same church. Moses is angry;
he's just seen the Israelites
dancing around the Golden Calf
and now he twists his beard with his right hand
and shifts his weight to the ball of his left foot
so he can jump up and smash the stone tablets
with the Ten Commandments on them.

I'd like to be that angry just once—
or, like Bernini's St. Teresa,
to pass out from pleasure! I think of Bo Diddley
as I scurry down the Via XX Settembre
and up the steps of the church of Santa Maria della Vittoria
with its great Baroque sculpture
in which the angel smiles at the saint
as sweetly as a child would, yet his copper arrow
is aimed between her legs;
God might as well have told Teresa
he walked forty-seven miles of barbed wire,
got a cobra snake for a necktie
and a house by the roadside made out of rattlesnake hide
because, really, the only question is,
Who do you love?

•

The lyrical, playful, slightly irreverent impulse to "Your Momma Says Omnia Vincit Amor" is fully formed in the title, with its juxtaposition of the colloquial "Your Momma Says" with the phrase in Latin, "Love Conquers All." And as the poem unfolds—thirty-five lines in four sentences and two stanzas—each stanza has a parallel setting in Rome: the church of San Pietro in Vincoli, followed by the church of Santa Maria della Vittoria.

One of the strengths of this poem is the incandescent rhythm, "oh but your loving is much too strong / for these chain chain chains / which were used to bind St. Peter in Palestine." I am interested in how the speaker, in gazing at great art of the past, wants to experience that intensity of anger, or pleasure, or passion that takes one out of the self, now. I think the last six lines have a wonderful surprise, as lines from the classic song snake back to the title and to the crucial question, "Who do you love?"

•

This is a poem variously about voice and voicings—with its daring quotations from Virgil's Tenth Eclogue and from Aretha Franklin, it proves itself delightfully postmodern. Maybe here the conflation of "high" art and "low" is more a deliberate matter of democracy; this is a highly democratic poem possible because of this age of easy travel between Europe and the United States. The velocity of this poem (and of the travel, for that matter) is exhilarating, as is its daring willingness to toy with a secular engagement with religious tradition. In a poem of apparent offhandedness and structural ease, it is interesting to think how Virgil was indeed to his contemporaries a religious poet, but what is more, after the twelfth century he was considered by the Church to have a "soul of the natural Christian" (*anima naturaliter Christiana*). It happens that Aretha Franklin's father was a powerful religious figure himself, famous for his sermons. I do not know if Bo Diddley fits into this mode but, frankly, I would be surprised if spirituals and hymns were not important to his early music training. This poem, unarguably, deals with passion and engages in a deliberate inspiration, a breathing-in of various voices intertwined: "I hear her say my daddy said come on home" suggests that home is made available or at least is revealed through a succession of sayings, or rather of sayers, each building on the previous.

Dazzling as all of this quotation is, I am finally a little disappointed with the ending. The velocity of the poem does carry us with energy and joy, but I still feel the largeness of the final statement as a jolt, a large claim finally unearned by the poem, merely assumed as poetic. Because we are carried so rapidly from the snake and barbed-wire imagery across "really, the only question is" to what the question in fact is, we are rather dared to question the question. And yet I think there are other questions. Still, the baroque qualities of "Your Momma Says Omnia Vincit Amor" are powerful and daring, and the felt spiritual questioning that rides along with each twist of the lines and the images makes this well worth reconsidering, which I will do next time I see it. Meanwhile I keep going back to those chain chain chains—the breaking of which allows us to move to the next line of Virgil's: let us, too, yield to Love.

•

Frankly, this poem did not appeal to me immediately. Like the responder above, I felt dissatisfied with the ending. It still seems problematic to me. The voice claims to know that "the only question is, / Who do you love?" but I do not feel that an emotion as strong as "love" has truly been brought into the poem and integrated into its dynamics. The weaving together of Roman architectural and aesthetic excitements, biblical detail, and American pop music from a distant era seemed facile, a little shallow. Thanks to the other writers here, I now appreciate the careful deployment of detail and reference; yes, this poem is "delightfully postmodern," and the collision of tones is a hilarious, well-planned train wreck.

The ending is particularly interesting. The "forty-seven miles of barbed wire," the "cobra snake for a necktie / and a house by the roadside made out of rattlesnake hide" form impositions from another realm of consciousness, detached from the external landscape and separate from the pop flotsam in the mind. The images seem ironically archetypal, drawn less from any literal landscape or mythology than from some surreal heart of darkness. Their strangeness is exciting, and it is unfortunate that after them the poem ends so abruptly and glibly. I wish that this moment had been "developed" more.

Still, this is a strong, original poem—I'd love to read more by this poet.

•

Over the years I've said to myself and anyone else indulgent enough to listen that there are two things an American poet should never do: one, he or she should never go to Italy and write directly about it; two, he or she should never listen to the blues (or jazz, or soul, or rock, or whatever, but the blues especially) and write directly about it, much less crib from it or adopt its diction. While blatantly stupid comments to make, they still hold for me something worth addressing within them, since the first often leads to some of the most pretentious, soulless, and obvious contemporary poetry I've read, and the second often leads to the some of the most boring; in both cases the imagination and diction of the poet is often clearly, sometimes embarrassingly, overshadowed by that of its inspiration.

With that said, I met this poem with a great deal of resistance, however silly that resistance's foundation. And what the poem taught me—reminded me of, really—is that the poet's voice, properly pitched, can do whatever the hell it wants and succeed. And this voice is very well tuned, especially so in the first stanza—overwhelming with its irony and grace any such resistance. As the lines and their diction intertwine, I want to join in the celebration—which is what it seems—of so much disparate experience coming home; I too want to "smash the stone tablets."

But the ending is deeply disappointing, as the second stanza seems almost to dissolve into the trope of the first with no interesting affect. The first line of the stanza, maintaining the energy of the first, promises a great deal: either to be "that angry" or "to pass out from pleasure," but neither happens; the narrator—so far the thread around which the poem's diction has been woven—mostly disappears, and Bo Diddley takes over. (Should there be a "But" opening the second sentence before the narrator scurries?) Without the narrator and her or his irony, I hear Diddley's song—especially considering its sharp transition from Aretha's—as a sentimental answer to the question the song itself, more wisely, I think, simply raises.

•

Maybe the only question is "Who do you love?" but what kind of love do we mean? The severe love of the Old Testament God? Moses' loyalty? St. Peter's denial? The strength and solemnity of Michelangelo? The ecstatic love of St. Teresa? The fluidity and wit of Bernini? All are expressions of sacred love, but the fun and inventive opening of the poem, with its yoking together of these images with words from two divergent profane love traditions (Classical Latin and the blues), sends a lot of plates spinning in the air; ultimately, though, the poem for me—as for other responders—doesn't end with a satisfying accounting of its impulses. The figures for love don't add up. For all the speaker's running and scurrying, the poem just stops.

•

The running narrative free-verse line acts here like a car chase or a foot race, and carries the rather incidental detailing—classical culture and pop culture—that leads to the subject: "the only question is, / Who do you love?" The energy is undeniable. The subject isn't entirely a surprise, since there is mention of other emotions that we associate with love or lost love—chiefly anger—but the poem could have ended variously. In a more postmodern postmodern poem, the author might well have written "the question is, / (X or Y)" in the same last lines. Some of those X's and Y's might read: Can you escape love (even by running to Italy); or Is commitment real? Actually, many of the details of the poem could be easily changed, and the lines, too, but the running free-verse line accepts this flux, and flux does create energy. It's a style of composition. Will the poem last into eternity? It may be a matter of conviction. If readers believe in offhanded passion or have felt this angry and helpless or been to Vincoli or love Michelangelo, then maybe yes. The permanence of the lines doesn't matter so much after all, perhaps. For those others, then, what keeps the poem in mind? Energy, as I said.

The surprise of a house made of rattlesnake hide keeps that figure in mind. A pleasing irreverence toward art and religion, if irreverence is part of one's makeup. That's a lot of reasons to like the poem, and all of them are summed up in the title. I don't think the poem goes far enough into art or emotion.

Honorée Fanonne Jeffers

BIG MAMA THORNTON

They call me Big Mama and I make
much music when I walk. I know
you want to find the easy way
down to these marrow-full bones,
but please don't mess me over.
Don't play me like a puppy, lick
my face then bark at me. Do
and the two-headed lady gone
have your address and your
unlisted phone number.

I weigh three hundred pounds
and all this is real, baby. Ain't
nobody else living with me in this plush
house of mine. This just some deep
country meat padding your ride.

They call me Big Mama and the ground
be strumming stones.
These fine hamhocks will knock
your black iron pot all night long
but please don't mess me over.
Don't play me like a puppy, lick
my face then bark at me. Do
and I'll cut you so smooth,
I'll be on that train to Chicago
before you even start to bleed.

•

It's hard to tell if this poem is a spoof or the genuine article. Makes me think of Lucille Clifton's anthology piece, "My Hips." So we have a fat black lady who both does and doesn't want to be messed with. Except for her body playfully described as "This just some deep / country meat padding your ride" and "These fine hamhocks will knock / your black iron pot all night long," I find the language quite banal, doing the work of culture rather than that of literature.

•

The work of culture *is* the work of literature. What else could literature do? This poem seems like an ideal one to illustrate the limits of this New Critical enterprise we are all engaged in. It is a poem that is a statement of identity ("they call me Big Mama"). Who wrote it matters because this gives us the clue as to the sorts of communities that the poem aligns itself with. This information might, although it also might not, help answer that question of whether the poem is a spoof or not. If written by a skinny man, the poem has a different meaning than if written by a large woman. I like how it keeps telling readers not to mess with it. I like the puppy line in there twice.

•

A curious poem, rather a mix of the authentic and the forced. It is a self-blason cum love plaint transposed and translated into an African diaspora zone. It does not sound like work by someone who is from the social groups (African-American, woman) that are being voiced. There's nothing wrong with that—if the poem is convincing. Persona work is a time-honored tactic. The first sentences (first 2 lines) of the first and third stanzas are strong, but the writer is then baffled as to what to do next. Hence this poem is somewhat forced, making claims to enter and possess this voice, claims that actually come out fairly coarsely and unconvincingly, especially in the middle stanza and in any number of metaphors in the other two stanzas. The puppy/lick metaphor really seems out of kilter. The "hamhocks" and the intense sexual metaphors of the blues do not ring true, as they are not done with a cultural ease and finesse but are clumsy and stagy, even vulgar in a voyeuristic way ("some deep / country meat padding your ride"—good grief). The line breaks show little ear for diction or the rhythms of declaration; the diction ("mess me over") is sometimes questionable. It makes me wonder whether this is a particular kind of parody, the kind one is used to seeing from Charles Bernstein (e.g., his "male mainstream" poems in *With Strings*), parodies that are somewhat deadpan, somewhat indicating themselves by a signature awkwardness to call attention to the old laid-bare device. Oh well, one can hope.

If this poem does, in fact, come from an African-American writer, I'd say that the poem has exaggerated those materials to the point of stereotype and would wonder why, what purpose this serves, and who benefits from this kind of verbal activity. Finally, this poem points up the problem of doing this whole "Hix anthology" exercise at all. The issue is not that the poems have no signature; it's that the poems are so blankly singular. There is no context of other work by any given author so that one could assess what one thought the projects of these authors were. This acontextual presentation of work is a limit to this whole enterprise. One has little sense of the stakes of any writer.

•

It took me some time trying to come to terms with this poem—a poem that appeals to none of my preferences in poetry. The language as language is not particularly interesting—there is nothing surprising in the speaker's tropes, there is nothing particularly strong in the suggestion of dialect. It does not play with or against interesting issues of form. It does not suggest complexities of thought or feeling. The poem tends to invite, to demand, respect for a figure to whom the poem refers, the figure remaining outside the poem, the figure assumed to be imposing and admirable in its psychology and personality. But I do not find the poem itself to contain imposing or admirable qualities in any great measure.

But I have kept going back to the poem, thinking that I am missing something important here. There is the oddness of "don't play me like a puppy," which act would seem to involve a doglike behavior on the part of the person addressed: don't you bark and lick my face. How weird. And then there is the strange claim: "you want to find the easy way / down to these marrow-full bones." The phrase "marrow-full" feels literary, self-conscious, and incongruous. In the end the voice is one of a woman, imposing both physically and in her emotional strength, who is fearful of being tricked—fearful that she is not as strong as she pretends. This is an interesting situation, but I do not find the poem rising to its own occasion.

•

I really enjoy this poem. The Clifton poem that some say this poem tries to emulate is "Homage To My Hips." I believe that there is room enough for a Big Mama Thornton's hamhocks as well as Lucille Clifton's hips in American poetry. I celebrate the energy and joie de vivre of this poem. These effective lines: "These fine hamhocks will knock / your black iron pot all night long" are reminiscent of the salacious contents of the containers of Roethke's "I Knew a Woman."

•

This poem has some nice language-energy: I like the "Don't/Do" hook that is repeated twice and the flat humor of the line "I weigh three hundred pounds"—I once weighed 285 pounds and have always wanted to announce that in a poem, because obesity is an American problem—but I wish the sentence had ended there before turning into a cliché. The particular sort of cultural type that this persona represents seems to be in front of our eyes a lot right now: the kid who won the *American Idol* competition, Ruben Stoddard (May 2003, for future New Historians), and what's-her-name's character, the lesbian jailkeep, in the movie *Chicago,* which I've endured now on *two* airplane flights. I had several students last semester who probably would have wanted to memorize this poem. But the clichés seem tired and familiar, the walking-the-racism-tightrope game not really shocking or comic but simply easy. There are no real political or even psychological nuances here. I think being an overweight African-American woman in our society can be difficult and painful. As a creative writing teacher, my professional relationship with the kind of student mentioned above is usually sensitive and complex: I know I need to encourage the tendency toward a particular kind of dramatic self-assertion and, in focusing the writing process toward real emotional candor, choose my words carefully. The attempt often fails, and I am made even more aware of the ways we all suffer the complex racism of American society. This poem seems to be about something else.

Bin Ramke

VERSIONS OF ERRORS

They return from the film to find themselves still
clothed but in love. Suddenly she remembers that in
1956 her mother left the iron on when the family
left for the movies one night. The house they
returned to might have been a smoldering ash, a
reduced mass of matter—the sadness of possibility is
infinite and yet the swallows' paths in flight at sunset
spiral ever more tightly.

I believe in the past the Japanese divided the day
into twelve parts which they named for animals.
And if the hour of the dog was the time to write
letters, I would think it would be late, say ten
o'clock modern time, dark in all zones, and the
letter would fill with coy questionings, like
inconsequent warblings of birds disturbed by the
dark. I should like my day to end so.

She loved something so intensely she never failed to
include it in anything she wrote. Whatever the
ostensible subject, Stein wrote only about her love,
her intensity of commitment turning language itself
ecstatic under her tongue. Her tongue became a
little bed, a pillowed redness upon which she would
invite day and night the body of her love to lie. Lie
to love, her body night and day.

Matter, from the Latin for material, stuff, wood, derived from *mater,* mother, orig. the growing trunk of a tree—the bark of a tree, too, is alive, especially the smooth such as aspen into which lovers like to carve by hand their initials, sometimes with entwined heart-shapes, and sometimes the tree is thus infected and if aspen the entire grove will die since they are all one tree manifested.

•

When one writes a prose poem, one is saying: "Folks, I really don't give a hang for form—this one's all about the words and nothing else." But the author of "Versions of Errors" presents a lightly kneaded version of the usual rigid prose format, so I began reading with hope. And my expectations were met, for the most part; this poem presents a number of very different errors, all treated with rueful whimsy. It's witty, it's surreal, it's my kind of poem—almost.

I think the author could have done two things to make a good poem even better. The first would be to eliminate stanza 3, which is coy to the point of excluding readers who don't worship Gertrude Stein (that includes me). And the second change would be to come up with a title that has more fiber content; "Versions of Errors" is pretty vaporous. These cavils notwithstanding, the poem made me think and, more important, argue.

•

"Versions of Errors" is choreographed into four tightly balanced paragraphs. The first three open with varying pronouns—they, I, she—and the fourth paragraph with its opening word, "Matter," brings it all together.

Of the four sections, I worry that the second has the least authority, with such phrases as "the letter would fill with coy questionings." Nevertheless, the fourth paragraph, with its opening etymology, its thematic return to the opening, its enormous divergence between "intention" and "effect," contracts and expands the poem in emotional power and resonance. Here lovers who intend to celebrate or memorialize their love by carving their initials into the trunk of an aspen might infect that tree and lead to the destruction of an entire grove. The power of this last hypothetical gives the poem a potent ending.

•

What unites the four sections of this poem? The poem's title provides an answer: taken together, the segments may well add up to a catalog of different types of errors. The first involves the almost accidental avoidance of tragedy—the slip-of-the-mind that could have burned the house down but this time, at least, didn't. The second involves willful poetic license—hence the subjunctives. The third error is hardly an error at all—a writer—Gertrude Stein—who allows herself to be seduced by the loveliness of wordplay from her ostensible subject, just as the author of our poem gives in to her own moment of wordplay at the section's end. Finally, in section 4, we see an error of egotism, willful lovers imposing their initials on a tree, not caring that the bark is alive. Their need to express themselves makes them careless, even selfish.

If this is meant to be a catalog, why stop at four? Surely the world abounds with versions of errors, but the poem's brevity—its refusal to be a catalog—hints that some thematic element ties these errors together and that there will be a movement—from something to something. However, the poem's movement seems arbitrary—if there's an organizing principle at work, I'm at pains to say what it is. As for what the poem is saying about error, that too remains obscure. Patterns threaten to emerge but don't. The poem's first line and its entire last section hint that romantic love and the errors it engenders will be our subject here, but no. If the poem is about mistakes born of the need for self-expression, what do I make of the mother's iron? I persist in wanting the poem's disparate parts—each compelling and sometimes even lovely—to add up to something more.

•

With its pun on eros in the title, we see that these are paragraphs on love and some of the classic topoi: desire, yearning, distance, nostalgia. There are interesting little thematic twists that suggest (for the most part) a muted matrisexuality, by which I mean an erotic yearning for the mother, not a sexual bond represented. In this work, mothers (including Stein) pull against other "lovers," which explains some of the wistful tone and the insistence on "errors" of "eros." Something that intrigues me is the use of sentence-based writing, but a general resistance in this piece to the disjunctive, apoetic contrasts of sentences that some contemporary examples of "New Sentence" or "poet's prose" mode offers. My sense is that the writer is quite aware of these contemporary avant-garde strategies, is consciously drawing from that well, but is also consciously softening and sweetening the strategies so they lose their (possible) abrasiveness. The writer does this not the least by an insistence on paragraphs of full narration rather than interrupted, distributed, or discontinuous statements of event happening, as one might find in experimental work.

The sweetening is marked not the least by a use of well-rounded cadences of high poesy in the sentence at the end of each paragraph (but the penultimate sentence in paragraph 3). This is signaled for me by the words "infinite," "coy," "heart-shaped," and some others. But a pattern that should definitely be noted is the insistence throughout on words beginning with "in-" like "infinite," "inconsequent" "intensely/ intensity," "include," "invite," "initials," and "infected." There are variants on this "in" phoneme in the pronunciation of "aspen" at the end. This kind of sub-rosa sound-work going straight through this text (as well as the repeat of words such as "matter," "swallows" and "birds," "lover") tends to hold things together that otherwise might fly apart. This brings me to a detour: Why do some of the remarks here on these pieces of writing act as if the text is being discussed in some workshop? "Workshopped" is the unlovely term current for these activities: the implicit "I like it" ("it's my kind of poem"), "I don't like it" ("It's pretty vaporous"), and "this is how I would revise it." The problem with this behavior when faced with a text is that it seems to try to draw the work to some understood or implicit norm of coherence. Not everything needs to go to the middle way.

•

I read this poem several times, put it aside, then went back to it. I confess I was more taken by the comments upon the poem than the poem itself, particularly the last response; the above reader's recognition of the pun on "errors/eros" and the repetition of "in-" sounds brought the poem together for me in a way that my own readings couldn't. Frankly, I'm still not convinced that all these paragraphs are successfully interconnected revelations about versions of errors or the potential error inherent to all eros—the poem seesaws awkwardly between an optimistic view of desire (lovers in the theater "come back clothed but in love" as the narrator recalls a house fire narrowly averted) to a positively pessimistic one (lovers carve their names on trees, hence effectively—affectively? another pun—killing them). In-between these two poles, hope in "coy questionings" and sensual ecstasy. Beyond this, there's little I can say except that the prose form fits very nicely with the poet's essay-like, anecdotal "pairings."

So I left the poem and began thinking about the project we've all undertaken with this anthology. Initially I understood we would be implicitly defending our own aesthetic through a critical reading of work from other poetic "camps." What has been made clear to me as the process has continued, however, is that I feel strongly for no particular school, no particular aesthetic, and that what I secretly hoped to discover in myself—a consuming moral or aesthetic outrage at a particular poem or group of poems—simply isn't possible. Partly it's the secrecy of the venue that makes such hesitancy attractive, but mostly I've come to see how few affiliations I have as a writer, and how often I have been encouraged by older poets *not* to develop these affiliations. No hard-won political, social, or ethnic mores dictate the way I write, no matter how intimately they shape me as a person; this is a result of witnessing the skepticism other writers have towards poetry that addresses or is influenced by these subjects. Consequently, I take what I want from a variety of aesthetics, cobbling together work that, to a much older or more "affiliated" poet, perhaps, might resemble Frankenstein's monster, true only to its own self-interested ends. Perhaps such pragmatism is the true result of American modernism, as James Longenbach and Jorie Graham have argued, or perhaps it's an intellectual slackness born more out of a general distrust and disinterest in politics, religion, commercialism than any rage at a rapidly fragmenting "canon" of poetry in English. What to defend for yourself *in* poetry when you can't defend yourself *out*side of poetry? I don't know. But I'm surprised to discover how this unwillingness to "affiliate" myself leaves me with a limited critical vocabulary, since instead of trying to place new work within a coherent (if not singular) tradition, my inclination is to find what I myself would steal or dismiss as device, hence intensifying the feeling of workshopping that the previous respondent noted. My poetic scavenging makes such qualifiers as "great" or "bad" in any *eternal* way hard to come by because for so long that hasn't been and probably couldn't be the question that obsessed me. It has, much to my dismay, hardly been an issue at all. Coming to this understanding is certainly one benefit of this project. Whether it has altered my perspective as a critic for the long term remains to be seen.

•

There's a lot going on in here, and a lot of substance in the critical comments the poem has accreted so far. (I rejoice to concur with critic number 2, who sees a potential catalog of types of errors, and with critic 4, who sees the poem "softening and sweetening" the New Sentence via "paragraphs of full narration"—or at least exposition—and "well-rounded cadences.") The poem seems more than usually self-descriptive (as critic 5 has perhaps noted too) since it describes not just purported errors but examples of the one/many problem: is the burnt house still a house? Is a day one thing, or twelve things (animal-hours), or twenty-four (modern western hours), or infinitely many (perceptual events)? Is a grove of aspens one thing, or many, and if one, is a grove of maples many too? What about a group of human beings? a family? a mother and her children? Gertrude Stein and her various writings (which, more than with other gifted writers, seem to make up a continuous project, a unity)? These questions come up but aren't answered (nor need they be); I found myself uneasy about certain self-consciously poetical conclusions ("Lie to love, her body night and day"), but largely delighted with the associative play—it's unusually musical, hence unusually attractive, for a prose poem. . . . By the way, has anyone else noticed that the whole poem could be a response to Frost's "The Need of Being Versed in Country Things," since it contains a burned-down house plus human nostalgia not shared by birds (who sing)? I should like my poem to end so.

•

I am matter. I am derived from mater, mother. Once I returned from a movie house still clothed and (in my diary) in love. My clothing was mismatched, but my innocence had stayed intact.

And there was a fire in my childhood home, and—yes, it's true! A fire in my mother's childhood house also.

I am finding myself in this poem. I am here and there and everywhere, and it is as if I am being in stop-time photography deflowered beneath a mirrored ceiling.

But why must I speak of this regretfully? I am not a thing as passive as a tree. No one dissects me.

Rebecca Seiferle

WHY I AM GLAD
THAT YOU CALL ME WICKED

When Simone Weil said it would be wrong
to think the mystics borrow the language of love
for it is theirs by right, though she didn't call it
the heavenly song of cock and cunt, perhaps that's
the inevitable conclusion of the sacred heart wounded
into a womb, an arrow in the hand of an angel
piercing such a depth in the body until it's beyond
what the body knows, delirious among the lilies
or tasting the sweet meats of that table. Yet
whoever the mystic woman is, she's not "about"
sex, it's not some sexual fantasy that she lies with
in the dark mansion of God, sleeping every night
in a different room, curling herself to the different shapes
of emptiness. It's not some narrative of first
he this, then she that, that makes her tremble,
being naked and open to nothing but the dark
night, that *noche oscura,* when with love inflamed,
the saint runs out of the house into the hills,
for she remains, asleep and dreaming, and in God's
innumerable rooms, innumerable forms and shapes
of love, she lies down with them all in the depths
of her body and blood, until every vision and icon
shines with a glimpse of the forgotten and atavistic
feminine body, pouring out of her as if out of the nipple
of that blue stone embedded in the miraculous

hand, as she herself becomes her own threshold,
no faces remembered or imagined flicker across the hymen
of her mind, for it's not a penis, even God's, that she
      imagines,
but the form of herself, the *knowing* of the body
of her own feeling, as in the Old Testament, it was said
that Jacob knew Rachel or Lot knew his own daughters,
the knowing of the body allowed only to men;
women, only the known or unknown, as she is known and un-
known but as she knows herself as she knows the other
that she is not: she enters herself, with fingers
of melting wax, of cold cucumber, with a thumb
of light, with all the abandoned utensils
of domestic life, with a stalk from the forsaken
garden, and with the lost wing feather of the angel
of death and with the voice of a baby's cry
nursing on the vestigial milk of the mother of mercy.

•

Aside from the awkward phrasing of the first five lines, this
poem attains a depth of understanding and exposition of subject
matter that only a true wordsmith can display. The chiaroscuro
of the lines about "the knowing of the body allowed only to
men" is reminiscent of Alicia Ostriker and Maxine Kumin. In the
sensual depiction of self-touch in the last five lines one can see
the influence of Sharon Olds and Muriel Rukeyser. One cannot
help but be satisfied spiritually and physically after reading this
poem.

•

A three-sentence poem with a foot in two worlds, sacred and profane. The poem brings the sensual into the sacred or the sacred into the sensual realm. A woman's love of the woman's self, in defiance of the male (the "You" in the title?)? Who are other possibilities for the "You" (God?), and what is the relationship of the "You" to the narrator defending her pleasure? How different poems are. How many cargoes they carry. How varied the vehicles that carry. It is poetry that is like God's house where you can sleep every night in a different room, mulling over important issues that surface for *mulling*. Poems come different as dreams. But on to the mechanics of this particular poem: free verse, compressed, condensed. I counted stresses, meter, and concluded: irregular. It isn't form as much as function: the message dumped in the reader's lap at a rapid pace. The *deliverance* of a definite message. The poem traveling like a freight train. The narrator in fast drive, moving on with abandon, seeking newfound mercy, an alternate source of grace.

•

The poem's sensuality is derived as much from the length and languor of the sentences as from the erotic reference and detailing, and the poem achieves a certain amount of its intimate tone in address, as characterized in the title. The speaker surely is female, perhaps the writer, though I didn't know this when I made these comments, and I was struck by the poet's distancing device of having the female speaker, the "I" in the title, who speaks to the presumed lover, male or female, argue her case from the third person. The "I" is "wicked" in the title, but the "she" in the body of the poem "lies down with them all in the depths / of her body and blood." The speaker is talking about herself by talking about "women, only the known or unknown, as she is known and un- / known but as she knows herself as she knows the other / that she is not." This is what, I think, probably saves the poem from sentimentality in phrases like "miraculous / hand" "lost wing feather," "voice of a baby's cry" and "mother of mercy." How differently the poem would read if the third-person pronoun were changed to first person, the writer was male, or readers knew that the female writer was gay. Readers work from a set of behavioral assumptions, which colors interpretation. Heterosexual, I assume the female speaker is speaking to her male lover, and then the lines in the final section, even the line breaks "forsaken / garden" and "angel / of death," take on a tone less of deep regret if the beloved was female (for having irrevocably "abandoned" male/female domesticity and the biological intimacy with a child) than simply of coming to orgasm without the potential, this time, for impregnation. Biblical references in the poem enhance either interpretation. The baby's cry, on the other hand, would take on two different meanings. Much would change, but not the fit between erotic content and sensuously conceived language.

•

This poem's strengths include a musical sensuality, a boldness of subject and point of view, an abiding insight, a psychological subtlety, and a sinewy syntax that for the most part gives urgent momentum to the meditative structure of the poem. It's true that the first five lines get clouded by the insertion of the clause "though she didn't call it / the heavenly song of cock and cunt," because the true reference of the contraction "that's" is subsequently obscured. The poem's argument makes most sense if "that's" refers to the clause of the first two lines. A similar problem emerges in the third sentence, where the clause "for she remains, asleep and dreaming" appears grammatically to modify the immediate precedent: "the saint runs out of the house into the hills." But the argument is most meaningful if we see "for she remains" as modifying the opening clause: "It's not some narrative of first / he this, then she that." So in attempting some of the poem's extremely acrobatic syntactic gestures, the language, in my mind, loses balance a couple of times. Nevertheless I admire the way in which the poet weaves narrative material so seamlessly and physically into lyric speculation, and the concluding section as a result is wildly satisfying and surprising. There is a significant feminist reversal here: an endorsement of both positive *and* negative capability. We see not only an amorous act of "self-knowing" and hence a reclamation of subjectivity, a self-affirmation in the form of masturbation, yes, but also the healing way in which she experiences herself as two people, the self and the other, the wicked and the sacred, the thirsty child and the nurturing mother. The experience of self-unification is predicated on that of self-division. And what she is penetrated by are the domestic, the forsaken, the angelic, the deceased—all potentially agents or emblems of estrangement, now invited into the realm of the body, redeemed, transfigured, mercifully, into pleasure.

•

This poet knows his craft (I'd wager this is a straight man speaking): the poem demonstrates strong attention to sound ("wounded"/"womb," "delirious"/"lilies," "fantasy"/"mansion"), an appealing, elastic, lineation strategy, a shrewd insistence on precise diction ("borrow" and "about" are pivotal to its argument), and a powerful rhetorical drive. This is clearly a poet with many resources. The poem draws me in immediately. Yes, the language of love is the mystic's by right, I say to myself, and Simone Weil still has much to teach us, but then I flinch, or perhaps some prudery in me does, at "the heavenly song of cock and cunt." It just seems too graphic for the grander reach of mysticism. And *song?* Now, that's some loud rogering! But, I say to myself, maybe that phrase is how others feel. So I continue to the end of the poem, and get taken in again and again by many of the poem's beauties, but finally, and after several weeks of musing on the poem, I think the poem is ultimately wrong about sex, about sex for a woman—at least my experience as a woman. If nothing else, this poem made me consider my own relationship to ecstasy and how difficult expressing that experience is for any of us: that's why we need metaphor, but to me, in the end, ecstasy doesn't seem to be "about" penetration of the body (and what woman—even a mystic nun—feels her body "forgotten" and "atavistic"?) Ecstasy isn't about "entering [oneself], with fingers / of melting wax, of cold cucumber, with a thumb / of light, with all the abandoned utensils / of domestic life, with a stalk. . . ." And yes, it's far beyond a "narrative of first / he this, then she that." For me, it's not about *entering* or *being entered.* In the ecstatic moment, thresholds become irrelevant. Ecstasy is becoming "delirious among the lilies": opening up, blooming. Now, excuse me while I go find my husband. . . .

•

Everything which is vile or second-rate in us revolts against purity and needs, in order to save its own life, to soil this purity.

To soil is to modify, it is to touch. The beautiful is that which we cannot wish to change. To assume power over is to soil. To possess is to soil.

To love purely is to consent to distance, it is to adore the distance between ourselves and that which we love.

Simone Weil, *Gravity and Grace,* tr. Emma Craufurd (London: Routledge and Kegan Paul, 1952), p. 58.

If you can't say something nice, it's better not to say anything at all.

Yet being a parent or a teacher gives a provisional license to be "frank," to be negative, even to be harsh. Provisional, in that the license is given for good cause to help you, for your own good, toward some necessary lesson. The license of a critic to be frank comes without provision, unless it be the good of the body politic, our collective aesthetic benefit.

In *Gravity and Grace,* Weil (1909–1943) asks not what it takes to provoke a person to violence but rather what it takes to provoke a person to nonviolence: to abolish violence by absorbing it rather than passing it on round-robin or cock style.

The author of the poem at hand conflates Weil's agape with his or her eros; Weil's theology with his or her fantasy. Or maybe not confuses; maybe it's like a schoolboy's cartooning genitals on a picture of the mother superior (an honorable tradition, no doubt, in which one desires to be called wicked when one is only playing at being naughty). Or have we entered into that territory that Buñuel and Pasolini imagine so vividly: the (self-)sexualized saint as ultimate object of male voyeurism. But whereas Buñuel and Pasolini were engaged in a comic yet blistering critique of the imaginary that led to the fantasy, here we find the hymen of voyeurism intact. The atavism we are seeing is not the "feminine body" but the primitive male sexual fantasy of the girl-saint as exotic other. (Why, by the way, "atavistic feminine body" and not *female* body except to mark the atavism of the voyeur, imagining he is looking through the hymen not into another person's mind but seeing only his own reflection? So it's a form of compulsory autoeroticism.) Weil is not a saint but a radical social-activist communist jew catholic intellectual philosopher poet. When she talks about the language of love, the vision is social, not carnal.

I entirely agree with the very last section of the first commentary on this poem. However, since I found nothing "satisfying" about the poem or its ending, I was disoriented by the comments made immediately before this.

The first commentator also mentions the implication of the structure of these reports, in which we write about the poems and commentaries without knowing the authors. From time to time, poets or editors suggest the value of reading poems anonymously, for example publishing a magazine without author attributions. It sounds democratic, as if this would allow us to read poems for themselves. But artworks, like people, are not self-sufficient but part of a series, embedded in contexts that give them not only meaning but resonance, depth, you might even say life. So what one can articulate here is necessarily restricted in that it cannot account for these other often determining factors. Prejudice may be avoided, and the extent of that, the implications of that, remains to seen. But (poetic) justice is sorely checked.

If this poem touches Simone Weil, it is because it abjures her distance.

Our distance.

Nick Carbó

GRAMMAROTICS

The angle of delight is best
achieved while rubbing

the pluperfect button
in tiny syllabic circles

while the glottal stop needs
firm accentual strokes

for copulative conjunction
to occur. The placement

of the preterite tense
at the entrance

of a lubricated sentence
assures the inevitable

apostrophe. However,
if the apostrophe occurs

prematurely the result
is then a dangling

modifier, also
commonly known as

a pathetic fallacy.

•

"Grammarotics" is fun. Readers who may also be writers guilty of awkward or too studied "copulative conjunction" may think the poem less a hoot than writers whose language is, by implication in the poem, more like free love; but in all truth, who cares? You can laugh or not. A joke is a joke. My favorite lines are "apostrophe. However" and "modifier, also." I am reminded of Adelaide Crapsey's terrific little cinquain "Susanna and the Elders," which ends: "therefore." The previous twenty syllables tell us of Susanna's complicity, as perfectly rationalized by the elders, making the "therefore" a brilliant stroke of language, logic, and syllabic structure. The author of "Grammarotics" mocks "rubbing . . . in tiny syllabic sentences" and so is left to make a similar gesture in free verse. Here's where the wit gets serious. The distinctions and combinations possible in poetry (in thought) are enacted in the two brief lines and commented on. The stuff about fallacy and phallus is for high school.

•

This is a pretty good example of a kind of poetry that leaves me completely cold, bored, unsympathetic, and annoyed at what this writer thinks poetry is for. The poem somewhat preeningly seems to see itself as smart, sharp, and seductive and has been calculated to trigger the response: "Oh, how witty and cute you are." In fact, it is calculating to a fault. What it does is leave me in a stony-faced rejection, a kind of revulsion that may be far out of kilter with its small demands. I reject the jejune already-squeezed orange of its labored metaphor—an analogy between grammatical terms and stages of sexual intercourse. This main analogy then winds up a mini-machine of little whirring cogs and knowing becks and winks ("pluperfect button" or "dangling / modifier" or "pathetic fallacy") that are prurient rather than charming. Its couplets are also mechanical, a formal pun that has little to do with real thought about line break and stanza break. Light verse can be a great pleasure, but this is "lite" verse, like an advertising jingle, simply a delivery system for an ideology that poetry really doesn't matter.

•

This poem both delights and frustrates. More precisely, it delights in spite of frustrating. More precisely still, it delights only to the extent that the reader does not allow it to be frustrating (so reading the poem pits delight against frustration in somewhat the same way that life does). To attempt to find a meaning in the poem by following through each metaphor is a futile exercise, yet the poem's consistent wit demands some acknowledgment. The poem deliberately pushes the reader into one particular orbit, exactly the same distance from every point, and forces the reader to circle in that exact trajectory, paying only one particular kind of homage to its smooth and clever surface. It's a hungry life, to orbit thus. On the other hand, the reader can choose to forgo hunger in favor of an appreciative chuckle at the poem's own appreciative, nondemanding orbit of homage to the language.

•

I have no doubt that there is room in the world for all kinds of sensibilities and that there are precious few truly funny poems in the universe. A good joke is a great blessing, at times in part because it frees us from the burden of making sense. And this poem sets out to do just that. It tells us to lighten up in its own way. While it is true that all successful poems, including humorous ones, thrive on some degree of tension, be it formal, figurative, syntactic, narrative, or otherwise, this poem depends heavily on the metaphorical play between surprise and recognition. And it is not without a certain charm. It is also the case that jokes that invite revisiting, that deserve the kind of attention that the poetic line encourages, are jokes that resonate—which is to say that they in some elusive sense "mean" at the same time that they tell us to loosen our grip on things. As John Hollander once put it, serious and humorous are not opposites; the opposite of humorous is somber; the opposite of serious is frivolous. Unfortunately this poem is the kind which gets smaller on rereading rather than larger. In such discursive connectives such as "however" and "also / . . . known as," the veneer of logic, which is itself lampooned, is merely that, a veneer. The joke goes only so deep, and so the mind quickly uses it up. The ostensible subject—the erotic nature of language—is not in the least engaged. In fact, the irony (perhaps intended) is that the allusions in the poem are so stable and simple, so soon to be exhausted, that the poem itself is not really very erotic.

•

Not to overburden the metaphor but, like many a would-be seducer, this poem has an intriguing first line ("the angle of delight is best"), decent foreplay up to a point ("tiny syllabic circles"), and okay technique that quickly disappoints. It loses me completely at the entrance to its "lubricated sentence," and I never regain my interest. I don't think it has anything to do with free love or free verse, it's just too wrapped up in itself, too eager to show off—and therefore deeply unsexy, its wit ultimately a turnoff.

•

Fun, but not as much fun as it could or should be. The extended metaphor likens the correct or skillful deployment of English grammar to skillful foreplay and heterosexual sex. To work well, the poem must actually describe both grammar and sex—that is, the language has to make sense on both levels, and sometimes it does: "if the apostrophe occurs / / prematurely the result / is then a dangling modifier" means both that if you place an apostrophe wrongly (in the syntactic rather than in the punctuational sense of "apostrophe") you can get a dangling modifier, and that premature climax produces a dangling organ. A poem that maintained this effect throughout would be impressive (John Hollander and Heather McHugh come to mind as people who could do it). This poem, mostly, settles for something much easier and therefore less impressive: it uses grammatical words to produce sentences that make sense only if we take them to describe sex—the vehicle loses itself in the tenor. Copulative conjunctions, accentual strokes, and glottal stops might all be part of a language—though not English—but how could a copulative conjunction like "is" require the placement of a written accent on a sounded glottal stop? What's a lubricated sentence? In what literal or rhetorical sense could "dangling modifier" mean (be "also . . . known as") "a pathetic fallacy"? You can use almost any set of specialized words to talk about sex if you want—you can even use nonsense words or place-names, so accustomed are we to reading between the lines for sexual content: "You'll have to get your Cleveland good and stiff before you can slide it through the Cincinnati; move your Louisville gently back and forth and you'll be able to bring your Columbus to Bloomington every time." That sentence works if we take it to describe sex, but not if we take it to describe midwestern cities; in the same way this poem describes sex, in a skillfully giggle-inducing way, but doesn't say enough about language—neither about its own particular terms nor about grammar and syntax generally.

If these sentences actually describe consistently and accurately some language and writing system with which I am unfamiliar (if, for example, Albanian has a grammatical term called an angle of delight, a "pluperfect button," a verb tense called "lubricated," and a copula which requires a particular written accent), then I take it all back and pronounce this poem a marvelous example of light verse.

April Lindner

THE RUBIN VASE

Suppose I say the hardest thing to say.
In a famous drawing two black silhouettes
gaze at each other, noses almost touching.
The viewer looks away, then glances back
and sees a different picture, a white chalice,
blank space between the faces seeping forward
to claim her eye. It's the profiles or the cup,
never both at once. The space between
two people—between us—can ebb or surge,
insistent as high tide seizing the shore.
Your fingers graze my chin, your body lowers
to press against my upward-arching body.
What I feel is that thin film of air
between our skins. These are the words that lurk
between the words I say. One day I can't
abide your touch; the next day I can't stand
its absence. Though the inner eye can't hold
two views at once, there's still the nagging sense
that with a blink the picture could change back.
Why should I say what echoes in my silence,
as if you've never seen the chasm between us,
as if, once seen, it could be overlooked.

•

I want to like this poem more than I do. My trouble begins with the first line, with the way it makes what immediately follows anticlimactic and is in itself a tease. I lose interest before its promise is fulfilled; I'd rather the poem go immediately to "the hardest thing"—presumably the lines "One day I can't / abide your touch; the next day I can't stand / its absence." (And wouldn't that read better if it were condensed to "One day I can't / abide your touch; the next, can't stand its absence"?) With this "hardest thing" up front, the metaphor of the drawing's changing perspectives would have more substance and become more, not less, interesting. There are other issues, such as whether the emphasis on "saying" dilutes the poem's impact, whether the metaphor of the drawing stands in as well for the attraction/repulsion as it does for the idea that "the inner eye can't hold / two views at once," and whether the final idea, that "the chasm . . . / . . . once seen" can't be overlooked, is strongly enough stated to counterbalance all that came before. A tightening of language-thought would help overcome all this; a powerful poem lurks inside this one.

•

As I consider this poem a curious thing happens to me—I become curious about Rubin. I know that it was 1921 when he first presented this, his classic illustration of the "figure/ground segregation phenomenon"—either we perceive the faces and not the vase, or we perceive the vase and hence the faces form the ground. Rubin went on to say "It has been found that the one that is perceived as the figure can be remembered while the other that vanishes as the ground cannot be remembered." Re-membered, re-constructed. In a sense, then, in responding to this poem my thinking reproduces the figure/ground problem itself: the very poem turns into ground, into the background against which the more interesting (to my mind at this moment) issue of the psychological implications of the original research becomes dominant, becomes "the figure."

But this poem does, to give it full credit, perform an interesting metaphysical explication of possible readings of the phenomenon, which I do admire. The poem as a "perceptual completion" may be considered a sort of metaphor for human relationships as completion, recalling even Diotima's story (of human bifurcation unhealable) out of Plato. And all along, visual versus auditory tropes become increasingly conflated, as in the sequence "echoes," "chasm," then "overlooked" in the final three lines of the poem.

•

I agree with the comments of my two predecessors, especially the first respondent's feeling that "a powerful poem lurks inside this one." Their arguments were a bit abstract, though: in a word, I feel the poem needs to be breathier. The lines should flow together, both to create the greater musicality we associate with poetry and also because this is a passionate poem or at least wants to be, though the choppy sentences inhibit the excitement. We've all felt this way about someone, which makes me wish I'd stumbled across this metaphor myself. (Hey, wait a minute—I just did.)

•

The poem seems labored and inarticulate, leaning toward blank verse but unable to accomplish its flow, the lines cluttered with articles, pronouns, and prepositions. The poem desires its repetitions to mirror its content, but "between" six times begins to sound like someone coughing in another room.

In *The Hidden Order of Art* (1967), Anton Ehrenzweig states that what is needed when viewing one of Rubin's double profiles is "an undifferentiated attention akin to syncretistic vision which does not focus on detail, but holds the total structure of the work of art in a single undifferentiated view." He goes on to insist that "the artist can unconsciously comprehend both alternative views in a single glance."

"The Rubin Vase" requires several additional drafts so that its lines might draw less attention to themselves and better serve Ehrenzweig's argument even as it means to debunk it ("the inner eye can't hold / two views at once"). I'm charmed, however, by the poem's earnestness. It means to say something worthwhile. Interviewed in 1956, Andrew Wyeth asked, "is it better to say nothing brilliantly than to say a great deal inadequately?" The answer, he knew, is always no.

•

This ekphrastic meditation troubles me in two ways: 1) the exposition of the first eight lines plods along, the speed of language unable to keep up with the speed of image (think how Jasper Johns takes on Rubin's vase across many canvasses, substituting the profiles with Picasso's or his own, extending the double-image conversation to other examples like the virgin/crone or duck/rabbit pairings); 2) the extended metaphor that follows the exposition reduces rather than enlarges upon Rubin's image by focusing more on the two profiles (the lovers) than the chalice itself (the chasm). The mystery that two can be either two or one but not both suggests a sacramental triangulation that the poem barely touches upon, opting out for a more touchy-feely lyric over greater critical inquiry.

•

As the sixth reader to receive "The Rubin Vase," I initially found myself reacting to the comments of the readers before me as much as to the poem itself: "tough crowd" was my first thought; my initial impulse was to defend the poem. This set me to thinking about the nature of our project here: are we a kind of virtual "workshop," engaged in the sorts of readings implied by that term and its traditional processes? Would I, I wondered, have read the poem the same way if I had been the first to see it? Does our "conversation" risk leading us to lose sight of the poems themselves as we respond to one another's comments? And does the fact that we make these comments anonymously encourage greater frankness and objectivity, as surely our editor intends, or simply less responsibility for our opinions? What, if anything, does this experiment imply or reveal about the current state of criticism and conversation about poetry in general? It will be interesting to see the final results.

As to the poem itself: the poems I love best tend generally either to range out from this sort of central trope or lyric moment towards a greater expansiveness of ideas or narrative than does "The Rubin Vase" or more fully to foreground the elements of sound, rhythm, imagery, and metaphor to bring to bear on that central conceit a more intense heightening of the language itself than is the case here. Having said that, I like the tone here, the sorrowful way the lyric voice weaves together tenderness and cruelty to evoke the complexities of love, the image of "that thin film of air / between our skins," and especially the rhetorical question posed in its final lines, which seems to me both interesting and urgent, the place where the poem begins to enact the bittersweet limits of intimacy it describes.

Philip Brady

J'ACCUSE

Here's the dilemma: The adolescent boy
rocking on the toilet seat, arms clenched
around his concave chest to numb his pulse
and focus on his immediate need to choose
between medicine cabinet mirror or water glass—
which to smash and how to gouge each wrist—
this boy, although he hums, although a wave,
blood-red, wells up behind squinched eyes,
can never meet the man who wants to save him,
though the man exists, speaks now, in riven voice,
haunting his tortured self from long ago.
The dilemma? How to blossom. Entwine
in self-renewing present, let the man
calm the boy's wrists, purr "accord"
into the ear of the continuum.
Moments at a time perhaps, they join.
Then the glass shatters, blood spurts.
And who has broken the mirror or the cup?
The boy, despairing? The man arriving
thirty years too late? No. I accuse
the forward rush and press of language,
applied like a shard of glass to the boy's wrist.
I accuse myself for rhyming the tuneless hum.
I accuse you, who thought to remain hidden,
Reader, consisting only of eyes and nerves,
and a fan of fingers probing a bound spine.

You, Listener, ineluctable—I accuse;
though you are restless, caught perhaps
in bonds of collegiality or love
or trapped in auditorium folding chair.
You breathe with me; you yield to evanesce
into the scene, calmed by this voice—
this promise the boy lives—veiling
and sanctifying gore. Now you are named,
perched on the crest of porcelain
between worlds. Speak, my Reader,
you are no longer dark. Lift
a glinting fragment off the tile,
pinch between forefinger and thumb,
slice vertically along the bluish line
up toward the heart, toward God
whom I accuse—God whose name
is Blossoming in Blood, He who confers
on every incarnation implacable need
to wrap numb arms around torso,
and yet to be released into unknowing.
The dilemma: within is contained All,
but what's needed to say *All*—
the loaf-warm palate, teeth,
the eel-like muscle of the tongue,
produces without meaning the word *Other*.
I accuse and stand accused of harboring
such sense as vouchsafes boy and man
forever separate. I accuse
the stream of time and self-fulfilling plot
of abandoning this boy who rocks uncradled
endlessly on the brink of blossoming,
the hum rising in pitch as he curls forward,

gurgling down the scale as he lurches back
to Original Unbeing, Primal Wound,
All-Encompassing Holy Ceaseless Pain.

•

"J'Accuse" offers a complicated confessionalism. While a purely confessional poem would take a stance of sincerity, "J'Accuse" insists on its own artifice. It begins by plunging us into crisis—an adolescent boy hesitating over how exactly to commit suicide. Just when I'm sure I'm in the realm of pure, unredeemed confession, though, things take an unexpected twist: the adult telling the tale exists in the world of this poem, albeit in a parallel universe. My favorite lines here address an interesting and universal question: it seems unfair, even criminal, that we can't revisit and reassure our younger, more tormented selves. This alone would be enough matter and enough art for any one poem, but look at the terms in which the poem declares this essential unfairness:

I accuse
the stream of time and self-fulfilling plot
of abandoning this boy who rocks uncradled
endlessly on the brink of blossoming,

By "plot," the poem means one's past as seen from the present, but the word also implies the necessarily fictive nature of anyone's personal history. From its tenth line on, the poem insists on itself as a made thing, a document, with an author and a reader, and not simply a cry of raw pain. Still, there's something in this poem that doesn't love art, refuses its false comfort.

The poem's boldest mood comes when the reader—or listener—is made to suffer the indignity of being the boy perched on the toilet, mutilating his own flesh. As the title hints, this poem's method is confrontation—it insists on the reader as both victim and villain. The confrontation dares me—forces me—to resist. Pushed, I push back. I resist the high drama of the beginning and the claim that I am somehow complicit in this boy's suicide attempt. I resist being made to suffer his humiliation, to envision myself sitting on a toilet holding a shard to my wrist. I resist the speed at which I'm hurtled from idea to idea. Despite all of this, or quite possibly because of it, I feel gathered up—cradled?— by the last few lines, which couch the boy's psychic pain first in physical imagery and then in grandiose abstraction. The physical imagery once again—and more thoroughly than before—commands my empathy and allows me to believe, almost against my will, in an "All-Encompassing Holy Ceaseless Pain" that for the moment might just as well be my own.

•

Some of the complexities this poem puts forth seem more interesting than others, some seem like scaffolding—holding the essential structure up but obscuring it. It's not artifice I object to, it's the way the artifice here obtrudes without offering insight or redemption. By scaffolding, by artifice, I mean the poem's repeated and shifting use of "dilemma," the shifting accusations, the address to the reader. Some of it feels clumsy, some forced. What I find most interesting is the relation between the man and the boy, which I don't think is plumbed sufficiently. I like the boy's squinched eyes, his hum, the rhyme with "continuum," the poet's self-disgust at rhyming his own adolescent pain. I like best "the forward rush and press of language, / applied like a shard of glass to the boy's wrist," though I find "accusing" it both falsifies and dilutes it. The poem strives to separate the boy and man, to make it a tragedy that the boy "can never meet the man who wants to save him," and allows them "moments at a time perhaps" to join. Does saying that the man has arrived too late mean that the boy's survival is an accident? Mightn't the man also feel, somewhere, that the boy, in trying to kill himself, had tried to kill *him*, and that their mutual survival is a miracle or due to some combined strength neither could/can quite fathom? And later, at the end of the poem, isn't the poet saying that the boy is abandoned by the very fact of his survival? This is perhaps the most intriguing idea in the poem. The poem, it seems to me, wants to be an act of rescuing the boy from the oblivion of his survival, the thwarting of his intent, but oddly it doesn't pursue the complexities of their relationship relentlessly enough to do so. The nuances of their relationship could be explored more thoroughly without confessionalism, with a finer, more pointed, and intricate artifice.

•

I.

dilemma: within is contained All, but what's needed to say *All*—dark. Lift a glinting fragment off the tile, pinch between forefinger and thumb, slice wants to save it, though the plan exists, speaks now, in riven voice, haunting perhaps in bonds of adjacency or love or trapped in folded carts. You breathe with me; smash or gouge each wrist—this ploy, although it hums, although the ear is all continuum. Moments at a time perhaps, they join. Then the glass shatters, immediate need to choose between mirror or water—the porcelain between worlds. Speak, my Reader, you are no longer Blossoming in Blood, He who confers on every incarnation implacable needs to back to Original Unbeing, Primal Shard, All-Encompassing Sleepless Rain. Here's the dilemma: rocking on the rolling ruin, arms clenched around a wave, blood-red, wells up behind splintered eyes, can never meet the rush and press of language, applied like shards of gore. Now you are named, perched on the crest of rune's wrist. I accuse myself for rhyming the tuneless hum. I accuse you, who blossoming, the hum rising in pitch as it curls forward, gurgling down the scale as it lurches toward the self-worn palate, tooth, eel-like muscle of the tongue, containing All or what's needed to say All—self-fulfilling ploy of abandoning this gnaw that rocks uncradled endlessly on the brink of yield, to evanesce into the scene, calmed by this voice—this promise the rune lives—veiling the ruin arriving thirty years too late. No. I accuse the broken shard from long ago. The dilemma? How to blossom. Entwine in self-renewing concave chest to numb the pulse and focus on wrap-numb arms around a torso, and yet to be released into unknowing. The thought to remain hidden, Reader, consisting only of eyes and curves and sand, without meaning the word Other. I accuse and stand accused of harboring such sense as vouchsafes said and unsaid forever separate. I accuse the stream of time and of fingers probing a bound spine. You, Listener, ineluctable—I accuse; though you are restless, caught in the present, purr "accord" vertically along the bluish line up toward the heart, toward God whom I accuse, God whose name is blood. And who has broken the mirror and the cup. The rune, despairing . . . The

II.

time and self-fulfilling ploy of abandoning this rune that rocks uncradled endlessly on the shard
poem strives to separate the rune and right, to make it tragedy that the neither could/can quite contain. And later, at the end, doesn't love art, refuses its faded comfort. The ruin "can never meet the rune that wants to save it"—the poem's boldest mood comes when the reader, Gentle Listener, is made to utter for herself. The confrontation that the rune is abandoned by the very fact of time and self-fulfilling ploy, that rocks uncradled endlessly on the shard, enough matter and enough art, but spooked with a finer, more pointed purr. Mustn't the rune also feel, somewhere, that the ruin, in trying to blossom, by "ploy," means one's indignity of being in language, perched on the fold, mutilating the so, without confessionalism, betrays a self-disgust at rhyming in its own adolescent thwarting at which I'm hurtled from idea to idea?

•

I like this poem for a lot of reasons. It's rather unlovely, but it certainly engages me. How could it not? So much poetry keeps its distance these days, whereas a speaker jumps right out of the middle of "J'Accuse" and gets a true dialogue going—unlike much contemporary poetry, as I say, but also unlike our current Manichaean political leaders. (A war's going on as I write this, folks; let's hope it's over now that you're reading these words.) The result is a real Whitmanesque who-touches-this-touches-a-man quality.

I like as well the way "J'Accuse" offers up something that's mainly missing from the public conversation these days, and that's something I'd call religiosity for the irreligious. Just about everyone is interested in the bedrock materials of the religious experience—life after death, heaven and hell—though I don't know all that many churchgoers. Poems like "J'Accuse" make it possible to discuss these matters without having to roll out of bed on Sunday at an hour that's um, ungodly.

•

Will this boy kill himself in the bathroom (and break stuff, wreck his "scene") or will he grow up to become the man writing this poem (hence, apparently, "sanctifying" his troubles in retrospect)? The answer, we know, will be number 2—yet we feel that answer can't justify the "adolescent" pain the boy feels in the scene this poem of retrospect depicts, and the poem derives its sometimes considerable powers from our dissatisfaction; the boy becomes a perhaps melodramatic case of general disappointment, dissatisfaction, with the falsifications and losses in 1) any instance of communication, language, linguistic representation of experience; and also in 2) any instance of growing up (since something is always lost, alternatives refused or shucked away, in maturation—growing-into is also growing-out-of). It's a powerful situation, certainly—as Wordsworth knew!—and the poem at times does it justice. I admire the mix of dispassionate tone and vivid description in the first six lines (the best in the poem). I love "slice vertically . . . up toward the heart," and "rising . . . curls forward," which work both anatomically and allegorically. I also like the poem's refusal to ironize, its insistence instead on dignifying the torments that (since so many of us know and remember them) fiction writers and essayists tend to dismiss as "inappropriate" (whatever the heck that means when applied to an emotion).

The poem belongs to the traditions of retrospective autobiographical meditation, of "confessional" verse, and of blank-verse meditations about God. It invites us to judge it as it judges itself and as its implied author will judge it; it succeeds in giving its ordinary yet quite painful boy the grandeur he sought in that moment of contemplated destruction and that the poem seeks for him now.

If I admire those aspects of its construction, I wonder how the explicitly religious language fits in—I wish I didn't know from the poem that the boy had been raised in a monotheistic tradition, since the monotheistic abstractions at the end don't seem necessary to the poem's central dilemma. (That's not a brief against monotheism, just a claim that some of the religious language seems grafted on, not grounded.) I'd like to see more about the boy, less about God and language in general. (Comparison poems: Wordsworth, "Nutting"; Hopkins, "No worst, there is none"; Jarrell, "The Elementary Scene"; Hill, *Lachrimae* (especially "Crucified Lord, you swim") and, in a different way, "The Mystery of the Charity . . ."; Thom Gunn, "Autobiography"; parts of D. A. Powell's *Tea*—Is this a male tradition?) I also see failures of craft, space for more editing: "gurgling" implied that the boy in fact dies (or vomits), when we know he survives (and if he vomits, tell us that directly); "this boy . . . squinched eyes," "haunting his tortured self," "how to blossom" seem to me inappropriately stentorian, and "the loaf-warm palate, teeth" just clashes with the far more interesting (to me at least) "eel-like muscle of the tongue,"

whose vivid attention to the boy's actual feelings and phys-
iology make it striking indeed.

•

I appreciate the incentive behind this poem, the fact that hap-
pens against its reader as a sort of battle, and the manner in
which the poem's artillery becomes more deadly, dense, and
harrowing as its forces encroach. This poem sets out with major
emotional stakes in mind. One finger points in the beginning,
yet by the end we find hundreds of fingers shaking angrily in all
directions: at the reader, at the poem's subject, at the speaker
(and therefore the boy), and at God. In this sense the poem
operates as a runaway train—the lists go on and on, as the train
pummels faster and faster down the tracks, its brakes useless.
This poem has several wonderfully distinctive images, but we
are not allowed to pause and enjoy them; rather, we must hurtle
along with the poem's emotional freight that comes crashing, at
the end, against the face of Pain as the Divine.

The project of this poem is interesting in that the speaker (as
I understand it) returns to himself in the past in an attempt to
save that past self. It is a rather more interesting strategy than
the one famously employed in Sharon Olds's "I Go Back to
May 1937" because the speaker specifically returns to the self
he no longer is. While we know that the "boy" has lived, has
not chosen either glass (or has, and survived his wounds),
simply because the speaker exists, we begin to wonder if this
poem really isn't about a very certain death—the death of the
self, or one of many selves. It is this fact that helps me connect
to this poem emotionally as reader. I want to save the boy too.
That is why it is so effective when the speaker suddenly turns
to implicate the reader. I don't see this maneuver as merely
sensationalist; I think it effectively reminds us that it is often
easier to ignore those in pain than to undertake the work
required to help them. The reader can, of course, be anyone: a
stranger, a teacher, the boy's parents, the boy's siblings . . . of

course, the speaker has allowed the reader to observe what is a sacred and private ritual, and it makes an angry sort of sense that he asks the reader to care to the extent that he or she would wish to enter the poem and help.

I will admit to being less interested in the poem once it begins to blame God and therefore to raise the stakes even further. This part, it seems to me, could be another poem or an additional stanza. The freight of the poem becomes so heavy at the point in which God is introduced that I'd almost rather the poem end there, at that very realization. However, the poem's language and rage are its strength, and I remained fascinated with the piece for quite some time after I read it. It certainly is spectacular, abandoned, and explosive. It also has a lovely sense of distortion throughout. A powerful poem with a serious agenda, it strikes me as rather remarkable.

Juliana Spahr

JANUARY 28, 2003

Yesterday the UN report on weapons inspections was
  released.

Today Israel votes and the death toll rises.

Four have died in clashes in the West Bank town of
  Jenin.

Yesterday, three died in an explosion at a Gaza City
  house.

Since last Monday US troops have surrounded 80
  Afghans and killed 18.

Protests continue in the Ivory Coast against the French.

Nothing makes any sense today beloveds.

I wake up to a beautiful, clear day.

A slight breeze blows off the Pacific.

It is morning and it is amazing in its simple morningness.

I leave the house early so I miss the parrots but outside
  the door I stop to listen to the ugly song of the red
  bottomed bulbuls.

It is so calm here and yet so momentous in the rest of
the world.

Amid ignorant armies and darkling plains, the news
has momentarily stopped trying to make sense
and the stories appear with a doubleness.

Israel said the four killed today were armed men and
were killed in a series of clashes.

Palestine claims they were shot in running battles.

Palestine claims the bomb explosion in Gaza was caused
by a missile from an Israeli helicopter.

Israel claims it was a Palestinian bomb that exploded
prematurely.

In the Ivory Coast some school boys sing, "France for the
French, Ivory Coast for the Ivorians. Everyone go
home. We are xenophobes and so what."

Others carry signs that say "Down with France, long live
the US" and "No more French, from now on we
speak English" and sing "USA, USA, USA" against
the French.

Later today Bush will speak.

How can we be true to one another with histories of
    place so deep, so layered we can't begin to sort
    through it here in the middle of the Pacific with its
    own deep unsortable history.

I left our small apartment which is perched at the side
    of a dormant volcano that goes miles down to the
    ocean floor, perched on layer after layer of
    exploding history.

It wasn't just our history of place but the contradiction
    of the US taking unilateral military action to rid Iraq
    of its weapons of mass destruction that entered our
    two small rooms and we just wanted to leave and
    get on with the day's mundanenesses—email and
    photocopies and desk chairs and telephones.

While driving away from our small apartment, beloveds,
    I turned on the radio. ·

Today on the radio, Christie Brinkley exists and her
    worries about Billy Joel's driving abilities exist.

A lawsuit exists where Catherine Zeta Jones and Michael
    Douglas are suing *Hello!* Magazine for poor quality
    wedding photos.

U2 spy planes exist flying over the Koreas.

Supermodel Gisele Bundchen's plan to eradicate hunger
    in Brazil exists.

Heart disease in women exists.

John Malvo's trial exists.

Aretha Franklin exists and a subpoena for her exists.

Hackers of the Recording Industry Association of America website exist.

Thalidomide exists.

Zoe Ball exists.

And FatBoy Slim exists but now without Zoe Ball.

Bronze Age highways in Iraq, Syria and Turkey continue to exist.

Renee Zellweger and Richard Gere, lead actors in *Chicago,* exist.

Cell phones and tunnel vision exist.

Cable problems exist in a crash in Charlotte.

A dismembered mother, the shoe bomber's letters, Scott Peterson's wife and girlfriend, Brian Patrick Regan's letters to Hussein and Gadhafi, 19,000 gallons of crude oil in the frozen Nemadji River, all of this exists.

The world goes on and on, spins tighter and then looser
on a wobbling axis, and it has a list of adjectives to
describe it, such as various and beautiful and new,
but neither light, nor certitude, nor peace exist.

•

This poem is touchy-feely in a prurient kind of way: the world
is very scary, why can't there be peace over there, I'm so lucky
to be living over here yet feel guilty about it. How can I enjoy my
boring life after listening to the radio, sampling this, sampling
that, skimming the surfaces of reportage. On top of that, this
poem lacks art, reads more like journalistic prose. There's no
complexity here, neither in its poetics nor in its politics. Very
American. A real bust.

•

What is dangerous about this poem is its combination of
suggestiveness (by piling up particulars it suggests there is
knowledge here, that the consciousness at work is aware of
things)—and sloppiness: "How can we be true to one another
with histories of place so deep, so layered we can't begin to sort
through it here in the middle of the Pacific with its own deep
unsortable history." Well, what can such a statement possibly
mean, as journalism, political rhetoric, or poetry? That being
"true to one another" is impossible in the face of history? All
history is deep, whatever that crude metaphor might suggest,
and all is from some perspectives sortable, from other perspec-
tives not. The job of poetry is to be precise and to be engaged
with complexity. What poetry can do that the *New York Times*
can't do is to find in language, to find in the complexity of

language, parallels and paradigms that enable us come to terms (marvelous phrase) with histories and hysterias and to avoid the histrionics. Or it does its small work inside the language itself without trying to engage The World self-consciously, confident that language is intimate enough to matter.

"Sorting through" means looking closely, bringing attention to bear. Cataloging is not enough. I am not moved by this poem.

•

I want to like this poem, and I'm drawn in most toward the end when the poet begins the list in which every line contains "exist(s)." The jarring placement of light pop-culture references next to war and murder references builds momentum. But I wish this poem had gone deeper—either in terms of language or in terms of "meaning." "January 28, 2003" is just too easy, too didactic. I think it is possible to write a moving political poem, but this poem is too conspicuous. It's preaching to the converted.

•

The intrusion of prose into the poetry of being that usually appears in a piece is the lead weight of the world news that pulls down the creative flight of art. So heavy the world has gotten it can hardly rise from its moorings in hard reality. Maybe this is the message the poem carries.

•

"January 28, 2003" does not escape its message, borrowed from "Dover Beach," and may deliberately cancel poetry to chide both Matthew Arnold and any others who take pains with language in the face of international distress. It's hard to be certain. The new century's losses are reported here like headlines in some lines, radio talk-show news, and personal observation. Perhaps the writer has lost patience with poetry to legislate any

carnage wrought by ignorant armies, surely his verdict applies far more surely to ours.

I'm not surprised that previous readers dislike the poem so strongly, but I think they're applying wrong standards; rather than reading it as they would read "Sunday Morning" (say), they might try reading it as they would read Larkin's "Homage to a Government" or Wilbur's "To the Student Strikers" or Pope's most topical verse. At the same time, I do agree with the detractors this far: the best, most worked-out political poems I know do more with patterns, more with language, at the end (even if they end in irresolution) than this piece can in the sentence that marks its end. It's not the Best Political Poem of the Decade, I'm sure, but it does plenty of work, and I'm very glad it's around.

•

This is not a political poem, but a poem by a prolific (I don't say "promiscuous") reader of papers, addressed to similar others. What this poem expresses is a taint of shame I think I understand. Perhaps I understand this feeling more than any "underlying cause."

The majority of even minimally literate people (or as good as) can, thanks to deforestation, and moveable type, and satellite communication, and media conglomeration, experience at least a sliver of this consciousness of living on a "dormant" volcano. Every morning, as naturally as breathing, I foreground that feeling for a few minutes. I drink my orange juice and thank my lucky stars.

I do not live in California, where the air is filled with oranges, but I can always, to my credit, get there. In fact, this morning on the plane I thought: What haven't I accomplished!

And sweeter still, as someone somewhere said, isn't it a lot of fun to watch a destroyer of fables become the victim of a fable?

Afaa Michael Weaver

THE FIFTIES

In memory of perfection, Marty

What a mother would want for her good son
She would not breathe to a neighbor, for her own good
Is perhaps not the dream of that neighbor,
That he will bring shining and bright grandchildren
In the afternoons and take them home in the evening
All smeared with what their mother would not have
Them eat because she is that neighbor's daughter,
The woman her good son should not have married.

Better the daughter-in-law of her dreams,
With the tidy hopes of a tidy home for her son
And her grandchildren. So much work to do,
This happiness for the son who is the sun
That is the light in her own sky, and that he will rise
To his own cresting horizon, blue in morning,
Tingling reddish blaze in the evening, his majestic
Sense of himself true to all she had him believe.

And to let him go to chance, some woman
She does not know and cannot interrogate properly.
"What are your senses about propriety, young woman,
And do you know he must have this, and he must have
That, and only I can know these things? Do you know
He *is* the good son?" This is the way sorrow grows
Until a mother's wisdom shows her the way.
Subvert with homemade candy to the grandchildren,
Subvert with sweet notes in Thanksgiving pies.

Tidy this, tidy that, and remember I told you
Because I am the author of the one good son.

●

The unique voice of this poem carries the narrative to unexpected places of intrigue. What is not said in the poem is more important than what is said. If there is a good son, is there a *bad* son in the family? The clause "only I can know these things" opens up the mystery of what these things are. The repetition of the word "subvert" implies a conflict in the relationship. The aura of the poem seems to be calm and collected, as suburban life was supposed to be in the fifties, but the underlying narrative suggests something ominous.

●

This poem attempts the difficult task of making poetry out of primarily discursive narrative, most of which is rendered in literal language with sparing appeals by way of metaphor or the eye or, in a slightly different sense, through the poetic image (more largely conceived by Paz as evocative simultaneity). The poem asserts itself sensuously in large part by way of the ear. Its musical echoes, the compression and expansion of its rhythm, its frequent emphatic spondees coupled with a satisfying sense of the line (sculpted hexameters) and line break (all the end words have significant semantic weight)—all contribute to a sense of the poem as carefully made. The one central metaphor in the poem, the son as "sun," is not terribly original or surprising and a bit drawn out, given the simplicity of its conceptual work, but the phrasing here and throughout the poem is highly elegant, giving the end of the stanza and sentence a rhetorical flair. The poem handles the significant challenge of an elaborate exposition fairly well, though the first stanza in particular is the most convoluted in this regard, the most congested.

In one sense, the theme of congestion (perhaps as opposed to the experience of it) is intriguing, since it coexists with the opposite theme, the urge to master and simplify. The complication of power relations dramatized in the first stanza (more than triangular since they involve the grandchildren as well) is part of what inspires a certain tidiness and desire to freeze time (a kind of repetition compulsion) on the part of the possessive mother. Such, the title suggests, is the unacknowledged shadow of the fifties in general—an overwhelming desire to control. The appearance of order is there both to mask and to express the darkness of that desire. To feed the mother's grandchildren such transgressive sweets is not only her way of subverting her daughter-in-law's position but also her way of feeding her own ego. The mother as "author" of the son (echoes of Ben Jonson here) gets mirrored in the authorial voice of the poem, insisting on the goodness of the "good son" with a passion suggesting, of course, irony and denial but also the son's complicity. He is the quintessential "eternal boy," basking, "believing," conspiring. His "goodness" therefore figures as the stuff of the mother's simultaneous projection and installment of a childish narcissism.

•

Is the epigraph ironic? It is hard to think of anyone as perfect; yet the personalized touch of the epigraph provides an ambiguous twist. The torque of the poem resides in the triangulation between mother and son and shadowy daughter-in-law. How much control does the mother exert? Her sense of values appears reinforced at the end of the second stanza, "his majestic / Sense of himself true to all she had him believe." Yet the end of the first stanza and the opening of the third stanza show her loss of control, "to let him go to chance, some woman / She does not know and cannot interrogate properly."

When the mother of the opening line, who becomes a grandmother, lets her grandchildren be "smeared with what their mother would not have / Them eat," the poem becomes darker and more alive. The contrasting forces represented by "smearing" and "tidying" make me think of suburban America in the 1950s. Yet the mother who is obsessed with order and tidying is not opposed to "smearing" if it suits her purposes. In this undercurrent, the darker, wilder forces of life begin to exert their pull and pressure.

•

How to take these (motherly) sentiments, these wantings and permittings and not permittings, which the poem's mother wants for her (good) son? Are they naïve? Innocent? Characteristic of the 1950s? Sexist? Dangerous? Dangerously attractive, to sons or to mothers of sons? After raising those questions, the poem dives into an admirably complicated irregular pattern of repeated words (good, neighbor, dream, daughter, son/sun, properly/propriety, woman, etc.)—at times it feels like a re- or mislineated sestina (and I wonder if it began as one). These repetitions (as in some regular sestinas) tend to hollow out or ironize the repeated words: does "good" mean what we thought it meant in line 1? Can we be sure it means anything at all? But the poem's larger ironies have little to do with individual words. There is the mother's desire never to let go of her son, to get for him or give him what she wants him to have—this desire (toxic in itself) conflicts with her desire to give him success, which means independence, which means freedom from her. (That's how exogamous societies work.)

Finally, there's the question of where the poet (better, the poem's speaker) stands. Sometimes (as in the first line) the poem offers commentary we're supposed to take "straight" (it's true that such mothers don't make their hopes explicit for fear of offending or competing with potential hearers, parents of daughters). At other times ("Until a mother's wisdom shows her the way," or "interrogate properly") the language has to be taken either as tongue-in-cheek or as free indirect discourse, voicing the mother's thoughts and the mother's terms. Learning to read the poem properly means learning to tell the poet's (the poetic speaker's) attitudes and beliefs apart from the mother's (and learning to separate their tones); that's why the end proves effective, making explicit the already-implicit distinction between authors (poets) and parents (mothers). Learning to let your son grow up means realizing that you are not the author of a person, that no one can be the author of a person as one can be the author of a book—not even a mother who serves both as creator and as mentor, laying out all her "wisdom" before her son.

•

The tone here is of authorial authority; the poem directs the reader as the grandmother wishes to direct reality, particularly the reality of the son. The poem's directive and authorial tone makes possible the last stanza's appearance of the speaker, the "I," who says "remember I told you," which cannot help but bring to mind "I told you so," something that this mother anyway would probably say. A number of lines are iambic pentameter and others are hexameter, which suggests the way in which the grandmother keeps attempting to overflow her boundaries into the lives and expectations of others, as perhaps the poem wishes to overflow its boundaries. But my real question is with the poem's deeper equivalences, for it posits that the author of the poem is like the grandmother of the good son. How is a poem, or this poem, like a good son? How is the author of the poem like the grandmother? Well, one could answer in a number of ways: in that directive and authoritative tone, in its sense of spilling over and into the boundaries of others and yet of always being checked or contained by the neighbor (who may, given the analogy, be equivalent to the reading public); and perhaps even the subversion of the grandchildren suggests the way in which the author, not finding the desired response for the good poem/the good son among the neighbors, hopes the poem will become a subversive message for another generation.

Still, I don't think the analogy is entirely successful. Perhaps because there isn't enough subversion, so that the conclusion, with its appearance of the speaker and its suggestion that the poem is "about" writing a poem, seems somewhat surprising but also disappointing, as if the poem settled into merely another sort of box at the end. This is also a reflection of my own expectations that an analogy should illuminate or reveal unexpected truths about each of the two realities it juxtaposes. And this poem remains a rather expected portrait of a grandmother of the fifties, and as far as poetry goes, the idea that the author is the father or mother of the poem is also very traditional and expected.

•

I am struck by the tightness and the made-ness of this poem. It is a controlled poem about control. And even as I got lost in the meaning of the first stanza for a few moments, I realized it was because I was chafing against its melody, its tightness. As such, the poem is amazingly claustrophobic. And deeply dark. It scares me to death and I like this about it. I like the equation between formal, poetic control and smothering, ambitious motherhood. The poem is dark on the fifties, on the era of hope and prosperity and family. And it isn't just the bad son that is both said and not said in the poem, there is a hint of critique of American prosperity—the rising red and blue of the son, the "majestic sense of himself" that the mother so desires. With a title like "The Fifties," it is hard not to read the poem as allegory for an era.

Annie Finch

THE WOMAN ON THE BEACH

for Wallace Stevens

She could cliff and order waves, if they were climb-
ing up to reach her touch, or curling in
with drowning, freezing, fingers. . . . She hears

the phantoms tooling over shale, their long
unrooting waverings singing the air
into her hands. Then, as she plants and pours,
learning her music, with no difference how

she seeds them out, or harvests in, or racks
the dark with her questioning, she pulls the caves
from sleep with her answering chant and noticing shore.
The waves won't hear her now; she won't feed them;

and it won't matter how she pulls them in,
gathers their green in seedlings weighted all
spiralling through, to make her bounded dream.

•

There are divisions here: bound and unbound, order and disor-
der, abstract and concrete. There is a subtext or undercurrent:

subdue and harvest. Only the fields are an ocean, or the ocean is a metaphor. A trope. There is an uprooting or rerouting of the elements: moveable cliffs, a crop from the water, a universe with interchangeable parts. The poem changes the properties of the elements the way dreams change the properties of waking reality. Surreal, seemingly disconnected. Gravity fields shift. Expectations disrupt. Serve another purpose. Gathering seeds from the water: maybe the seeds are the beads of water that spray after the waves hit. Whatever the point, the reader moves the immovable and renegotiates the intentionality of nature. If poetry is to make experienced more than it is, what is happening here? The lines are not always clear; not the lines of the prose poetry, but the lines of expectation, the law, the order according to which things work. *The uprooting waverings that sing the air into her hands.* The categories move over a notch. The triangle is lifted from the billiards, after which the balls are free. There is an echo of that old fall, which makes way for the language as redemption. The title gives mooring. There is a woman walking on the beach. Through her, the reader enters an imaginative world of phantom waves, and rows of harvest beating the shore. But there is further change. The waves no longer hear. They won't be fed. What is to be realized? There are only slabs against which the waves hit? An absence of solace?

•

Robert Bly has referred to his early poems as "free verse with distinct memories of form," and this poem gestures toward the formality of the sonnet, with its fourteen (mostly) decasyllabic lines of (mostly) iambic pentameter and its occasional end rhyme ("hear"/"air," "pours"/"shore," "them"/"dream"). Each line seems to divest itself of density through its reliance on monosyllables, yet density accumulates despite the simple diction, mainly through allusion and idea. For example, "she pulls the caves / from sleep" echoes the second line of Bill Knott's two-line poem, "Sleep"—"Its caves come out and carry us inside"—and the title, "The Woman on the Beach," coupled with its dedication, intentionally evokes Wallace Stevens's "The Man on the Dump" in which "The green smacks in the eye, the dew in the green / Smacks like fresh water in a can, like the sea / On a cocoanut. . . / . . . how many women have covered themselves / With dew, dew dresses, stones and chains of dew." This woman, who "gathers [the waves'] green . . . / . . . to make her bounded dream," immerses herself in elemental imagery to begin "learning her music," to script her dream of density (Stevens's "The the") with such simple gestures, "singing the air / into her hands" as both nature and poetry have taught her to do.

•

A failure of imagination is what is described in the sonnet's last lines: "The waves won't hear her now; she won't feed them; / and it won't matter how she pulls them in, / gathers their green in seedlings weighted all / spiralling through, to make her bounded dream." The woman tries hard enough, ordering, hearing, planting, and pouring, "learning her music," but it appears that "to make her bounded dream" something more may be required, something more than the process of making that is suggested by all the participles and other -ing endings. The artificer in "The Idea of Order at Key West" could perhaps tell. Stevens has said in this poem, in "Domination of Black," all through his poems, really, and in *The Necessary Angel* ("its [the imagination's] power to possess the moment it perceives—as if we were speaking of light itself. . . . Like light, it adds nothing but itself. . . . It colors, increases, brings to a beginning and an end, invents language. . . .").

And another clue to an answer can perhaps be found in "The Man on the Dump," where the dew on the green and the "dew, dew dresses" of women seem a comment on women's freshness, yes, but "the freshness of night has been fresh for a long time," and "the green smacks in the eye." As the women in the poem cover themselves with so much dew, something bordering on sentimentality. In "The Woman on the Beach," that the waves in the first lines come "curling in / with drowning, freezing, fingers" seems a comment on the women's sentimentality, which Stevens's artificer overcomes, making of the "tragic-gestured sea" and "theatrical distances" something "of ourselves and our origins." The notion, too, in the last lines, that the waves could "hear her now" but "won't" is symptomatic of a sentimental approach to the material world. Stevens says: "the sea, / Whatever self it had, became the self / That was her song." The implication in "The Woman on the Beach," by way of the author's several allusions to Stevens, seems to be that no liveliness of diction ("cliff" as a verb, "tooling" with its tonal shift, etc.), adherence to a form, metaphysics, or poetics can overcome imaginative and emotive failure.

●

I admire much about this poem. The technique is flawless: the iambic pentameter gives the lines a tight, concise forcefulness that contrasts dramatically with the rich complexities and ambiguities of the symbolic "narrative"; the diction is flawless in its accuracy and surprise. This poem is interesting to the imagination. The colorfully abstract landscape recalls many Stevens poems, yet the weirdness and unpredictability of the imagery and so on seem more Blakean than Stevensian. The neatly boundaried relationship between woman and sea of which we hear in "The Idea of Order at Key West" is somewhat more emotionally neutral than the grasping, playful, futile interaction here described. Actually, the style and aspects of the metaphysics of this poem remind me most of some of the best poems in Ashbery's *Some Trees*, with the difference that the thematic concerns of those poems are formalist and post-Romantic, whereas this poem is bravely "psychological."

●

The language here, the meter, the small surprises of "cliff and order waves" or "seeds them out," are most engaging. The poem is so accomplished in its music that it could lull the mind to sleep, and yet, since it seems to be a metaphysical poem, I find myself perplexed by its argument. Why is it that she "could cliff and order waves" only "if they were climb- / ing up to reach her touch, or curling in / with drowning, freezing, fingers"? This suggests that her power of ordering would exist only if the waves had some human agency to touch or die. And yet the poem goes on to say "She hears / / the phantoms . . . singing the air / into her hands," which, while it is a diminished agency (as a ghost may be said to be a diminished agency of a living human being), still grants the human agency that the first few lines denied. By the conclusion of the poem, I came to feel that its argument was that the powers of the singer are simply to make her own "bounded dream," that there is no correspondence between her song and the natural world: "The waves won't hear her now; she won't feed them." She "plants and pours / learning her music," but it makes no difference to the waves, "no differ- ence how / / she seeds them out." This singer seems caught within her own dream, where what she is engaged with are the phantoms, perhaps all that is left of the natural world or the idea of correspondence with it, or herself, that subconscious "caves / from sleep" where the "answering chant and noticing shore" are only *hers*. As such, I read this poem as a kind of refusal of Stevens's idea of the poet's song as ordering the natural world.

•

This is dedicated to the ghost of Jacques Cousteau, whose dis- embodied voice first seduced me down to where the sunlight hardly penetrates, eons before I knew who Wallace Stevens even was.

I don't apologize that I have ever since childhood been too busy to enter further into any scientific exploration of those depths.

A lot of attention has been focused on the sea—by literature and other leisurely activities no less than by commerce and the genre of the popular-science documentary.

Sea, thou art sick. But will you ever be as empty as the rose? My child asks me: Why is there a boot among the fish in my magnetic fishing game? So much is thrown into the sea.

I read this poem closely and I went to see the sea, to see if there was even a single molecule still viable, a tiny space inside receptive to another load. But on the boardwalk everything was slippery with repletion—everything was full and fulminating, fried and heat-lamped, dead and heat-waved, piling up and spilling over—and I'm still, working at my keyboard here, a little nauseous and greasy with corn in my teeth, and the Coronas and the mangos on sticks and cotton candy are dominating my memory.

That sparkly air! So much extraneous desire accumulates.

Stephen Burt

THE NEW ROCK JEN

at 9
pm tonight kicks out
slow burns, betrayals, anything the Chills
complained about, & buries them as evergreen
news stories might be
buried & she can get on

(O polychrome) & go out; new jewel tones,
recombinant noise, cool tomes, floor toms, some steep
raked stage's cornucopia of dates
& pomegranates, grasshoppers or
metropolitans, become her: now Interpol search
for her and not the reverse,

& there is that half-finished grid
still going up at Ninth and 43rd (O streaky sunset, analog
eve) where something to see
has been seen through & will
be overcome. Avenue lights
entice all the more in the mist,

& though Godfrey adheres to the old
& admires a stranger just once in a decade, the new
rock Jen whose flair or
flare
of secrets nobody can hold
all by herself, moves once—

O sneakers, O velour
accessories—into her non-
stop plan (*each evening
the sun sets in 5 billion places*) under
ground, making the B
line work for her, out under the slangy sky.

•

"The New Rock Jen." What to make of her? She's fun to read, hard to catch or even slow down, what with Interpol looking for her, what with her secrets "nobody can hold / all by herself" and her "non- / stop plan." Is she a spy, dancer, prostitute, Web surfer, robot, alien, showroom dummy come alive, rock star, bartendress, model? She's city, that's for sure, and too hip for me, too cool—I can't get her attention to read her at all. God-frey? The Chills? Is she a fragment here, just part of what will be a sequence that will fill out her "polychrome" nature? Right now, as is, she's all velocity, and I won't want to stay in touch with her. As lyric, she's unrealized jazz and suggestion. Jen is rushing to the subway, where such songs whoosh and flare and disappear.

•

Slangy sky, you betcha! I'm with respondent 1, attracted and bewildered. Having no student or younger colleague handy to translate the slang ("evergreen / news story"? "floor tom"?), I cheated and Googled the title (no hits—but as one might guess, there are a lot of Jens in the rock world) and The Chills (which many responders probably already know is a band—from New Zealand, I think) and thereby learned just about nothing the poem didn't already tell me. The poem's sounds and their associations create its major generative principle, so we have Rock Jen (rock-gem), new jewel tones, cool tones etc. leading to the "dates / & pomegranates, grasshoppers or / metropolitans" (the latter, I'm gathering, is a cocktail, like a grasshopper or a cosmopolitan) which leads us—why not?—to Interpol. Once I swing through the impossible grammar of "not the reverse" (not the reverse as in reverse syntax? as in "her search for Interpol" not!), I feel the poem opens relatively easily into an exploration of process and perspective, and though (as usual) I don't understand the words to the song, I think I'm liking it and feel like dancing.

•

What a wonderful rendition of post-beat gothic gotham logos riding we have here in this vatic exhumation of place. Should the reader glean pearls of wisdom or lupine luxuries from this poem? Oh, just let it be and let the engine's energy vibrate between one's legs.

•

This poem is very technically astute, and while it primarily concerns surfaces, its own surface is pretty dazzling. I like how the enjambment enforces the sense of constant movement— and I believe that this poem is essentially a portrait of a young woman's freedom to move through the city according to her own "non- / stop plan." Isn't this somewhat crucial—that a young woman can walk freely through a city at all hours? The setting for the second stanza is a club—there are drinks, dates, and music—of course she doesn't stay for long. It's a poem about youth, strut, and independence. While I don't find myself deeply involved as a reader, I accept that this is not a poem of meditation; rather it is a poem about distractions, movement, and escape. This is a clip from just one of the five billion places where the sun sets.

•

First a paraphrase of sorts and then a fade into a more critical assessment of "The New Rock Jen."

"The New Rock Jen" sets the center of a light as the recombinant possibility of all things, or the center of a single sound as the recombinant possibility of all things, or the center of the recombinant possibility of all things as the center of all things. The poem strives to exist in real time. Those moments become a woman seeking the heart of vitality, a kind postscript to 9/11, that kind of carpe diem.

The challenge the poem puts to itself is to be both thing and action, matter and energy. The first stanza turns the words into squares in a Rubik's cube, where the things kicked out by the night are also active events in the "New Rock," beyond Tina Turner Mad Max Road Warrior. In that way it rocks. Jen is the emergent hero defying the Interpol Google because she is so much there, so resplendent in the process of being.

The performing space is the night awe of the city in its perpetual state of construction, the "streaky sunset" as analog, as much the eve of the lighting of dashboards in livery luxury cars as the adjustment of the eye to the oncoming neon, the sustenance of the nightlifers rising from the day-long sleep.

There is a Godfrey to the Jen as there was an Ike to Tina Turner, but this is not his moment. He does not have the resurgent hope of Jen, whose "flair" is also "flare." Perhaps it is the fire thrown to the sky to tell the city of this posttragic era of which she is the siren as siren, blaring the sound to announce a culture of sleepwalkers.

If Jen took breath before the tragedy, it does not matter. In fact, it raises her heroic status to prophet, the enlightened and hence weighted spirit announcing a vision she herself cannot explain. Prophets are only vehicles. If Jen is indeed posttragic, then she is also prophet. The culture of sleepwalkers is the sum of what comes after that Zero of The Tragedy . . . the sum of zero becomes "O polychrome."

The performance mode of the poem, which is to say the way it both lends itself to a dramatized reading and seeks to represent performance, lifts it away from the responsibility of more conventional ways of weighing the line. It works as long as I ride the energy of the action while reading the poem. In the first stanza, my eye is annoyed by the placing of "Chills" at the end of the third line. My tendency is to want to rest more there, but the feeling of the word "chills" does not quite do for me what the poet perhaps wanted it to do—to chill you into slowing down and to set the stage for evergreens, all of which attempts to give an ironic contrast to the city's landscape in the contrapuntal positioning of rural and urban. Jen is certainly not the country bumpkin, but there is that innocence about the poem's central figure.

It is as if the poem is offering only one effective reading of itself, namely a rock-music kind of dramatized performance.

What is admirable is also perplexing. Or should it be that way? The "slang" atmosphere the poem seeks to create is coming from an informed consciousness. This is an erudite walk through mid-Manhattan, and that mixture of erudition and even a slightly pristine gaze makes it a bit incredible. However, I am not sure if that false tone is not the source of the poem's playfulness and hence its joy or if it is the mark of an impasse, an inability to get more at Jen, whether she be real or fantastic.

"[C]ool tomes" say more on that matter.

There is the rhetorical air, which is perhaps coming from this tension between the erudite and pristine and the worldly. The second stanza comes to mind here, "raked stage's . . . & pomegranates." Is this a Victorian-era "New Rock Jen"?

I want more contemporary urban grit. I am not satisfied here to think that erudition gives a sense of continuity and hence timelessness. After all, we do have "velour / accessories." The preponderance of harsher vowel sounds lends another tension to a subject that suggests a festive tone. The pitch of the vowel sounds is lower, closer to zero ground.

Where is flight's soprano? How can we, in that way, see? Are the "sneakers" the winged propulsion units of "The New Rock Jen?" Could that be appropriate to the burns and chills of America's apocalyptic tragedy, if indeed that is what the poem references?

There is a somber undercoating to the poem that belies its playfulness. The language speaks to a heaviness even as it lets Jen trot out along an urban setting that might or might not be Manhattan.

If the victory is to throw away concerns of the "genuine" along with "hierarchic constructions" then the poem is liberating. I am just not sure of this subversive power.

Moreover, if this is not Manhattan, it does not matter. What matters is not Manhattan. What matters is that five billion sunsets are present and accounted for when the roll call sounds in the evening.

Finally, what matters is that "The New Rock Jen" doth rock.

•

What have we here? A rock DJ tired of spinning the Chills? A wannabe riding the subway to the periphery of Times Square? Jen's on a roll. Sporting sneakers and velour accessories, she emerges to misty lights and a "slangy sky" (nice image). Unfinished buildings streak the sunset, trump the view—lights, action, Interpol! "Get on" with your "non- / stop plan" and go, girl!

Carol Moldaw

CONDUIT

Because the branches of the tall trees surrounding us
are winter bare, the moon has been able to project
its luminance more than usual these past few nights.
I went to bed thinking about the Pashtun word
that translates as "man-with-no-penis" and means
"man-who-doesn't-beat-his-wife," but woke up
thinking about a writer I used to know, a woman
whose re-marriage was featured in the Sunday *Times*.
In our courtyard, above the spindle-tip branches,
the moon looked sublime, unfazed by footprints
and flags, the cost of reflecting back to us our secrets
from the one side of its surface ever available
to be read into. Once, on a transatlantic red-eye,
eye level with the moon, I stayed awake all night
leveling with myself, my life stripped clean
under the discipline of her indifferent gaze.
—O Moon, what I want back now is not my naïveté
but my nerve, through which your implacable waves ran.

·

Some poems, by grace, threaten to steal something precious. Of
course, these poems don't work by excision or explosion, and
"Conduit" calms us with the trimmings of a traditional medita-
tion: winter moon, tall branches viewed from a bedroom by the

speaker and (perhaps?) a lover. But even as the branches stretch, with our credulity, to touch Pashtun etymology, a reported marriage, a plane trip, and a moon which fibrillates from muse to reference point to landing site to interlocutor, and finally to pure wave, still a sprinkling of poeticisms like "luminance," "spindle-tip," and "sublime," soothe, whispering, "this is just an overgrown sonnet—see, there are the branches and a silent lover and the moon and a secret and sleep as agency of transformation—don't fret, it will come together in the end." Meanwhile, the planes and news and footprinted, gazing moons do not coalesce; in fact, their failure to assemble, so pointedly contrasted with the traditional devices of the poem, provides the means by which the poem steals (or steels?) our autonomous, unmoonlit, composed, expectant selves—our nerve—an act that seems with each reading less like theft, more like unburdening.

•

I love the stream of images in this poem, which takes us from moonlight to bed to performance anxiety (inability to give pleasure or inflict pain) to a yearning for the courage to embark on a new life (work)—all this, while the other half of "us" lies dormant. And the moon (Muse)—deceptively virginal, but wise; reflecting us back to ourselves in a purer, more courageous light and, with luck, granting us permission, inspiring us to take the plunge.

•

The poem is supplication for the nerve to see and assess honestly. Interesting—nerve as a conduit—to call what is, what it is. The poem *conduits* on other levels too—in the case of literary technique—there is the conduit of alliteration or word-likeness carrying sound through the lines: branches, bare, and bed; unfazed, footprints, flags, and reflecting; secrets, side, and surface; discipline and indifferent; naïveté and nerve—there is the repetition of words or word phrases: red-eye and eye level, eye level and leveling—and the repetition of thought: winter bare and stripped clean. There also is the necessary disruption in the conduit of smoothness in the movement from the first to the last of the poem: "I went to bed thinking about the Pashtun word. . . ."—the complexity of the implication that a man should use his power to dominate or it is not power. There are political aspects buried here. The moonlight more abundant because of the starkness of the landscape. I first typed eruption for disruption. But there is that too. The transatlantic flight zips the reader across the earth running waves of the moon. Moon runner. Moon as a small white sea. The alliteration of the waves. I clipped a short piece from the newspaper about John Ashbery (I didn't date the piece or note the newspaper) in which he said something about the privacy of his poems being about everyone's privacy. The transcendent aloneness in the poem. The inner secrets always with us.

•

This poem derives its mercurial lyric power from a sense of both immanence and evasion, a quality so characteristic of dreams, of territories dominated by the sensibility of the moon. Here the moon conjures not only an intimation of the sublime, of what is lost, what is longed for, undeclared, but also the indifferent gaze, the baldly honest, that wintery awareness that shines through the trees stripped down to their essentials. In short, the moon sheds an unconscious light. It is that place "unfazed by footprints / and flags," the buried self beyond the pale of power claims, of ego defenses and denials. As such, the moon embodies both wish-fulfillment fantasies and the force of the genuine, both the otherworldly (hence the sudden, self-consciously exotic diction of "luminance") and what is defiantly of this world, defiantly authentic, disciplining the speaker to a kind of emotional "leveling."

Moreover, it appears that the experience of the sublime requires a version of emotional discipline. One of the poem's most original, uncanny, and kinetic images is that of viewing the moon at eye level while traveling in an airplane, speeding and yet seeming never to advance, longing to span the transatlantic distance between the eye (the "I") and that aspect of the psyche which makes a claim on us, which is larger than us. What is left out in the poem, in spite of the speaker's sense of confronting the facts, is simply that, the facts. Certain distances are never bridged. What we get are fragments under the pressure of urgency and denial. And the poem is far more evocative, more curious, for not having violated its tone with expository narrative. We can't even say for certain whether the "man-with-no-penis" haunts this speaker because he may be such a man in some ways or that he fears such a man or being such a man (the poem's speaker could even be a woman, for all we know). At any rate, something appears awry with the speaker's erotic relationship to an individual or the world at large, something echoed in images of lost potency, lost connection, of consequent anger or guilt. Hence the mention of remarriage, in addition to reminding the speaker of a lost personal association, offers a flicker of possibility—albeit someone else's—some intimation of the new, the *Times,* what resonates with the speaker's desire and dread. In longing for connection to others, the speaker must first become vulnerable and open that primary "conduit," the connection to the moon, to the Self and its uncontrollable waves "running" (is it in anticipation or flight?) out of the secret, the wintering, life.

•

I think the first commentator hit the nail on the head in calling this "an overgrown sonnet," couplet and all. (It even has those visual-pentameter line-lengths.) And in fact, my feeling is that the first three lines could be lopped off with no harm whatsoever to the poem, and with some benefit. (Okay, that leaves fifteen lines, but that's pretty darn close. . . .) The first three lines have little to offer in terms of image or music, and most of the information is repeated elsewhere (the bare branches become "spindle-tip branches"). "[T]o project / its luminance more than usual these past few nights" crosses the thin line from plainspoken to prosaic. The only reason that I can see for keeping the current opening is the "us"—an implied second person haunting the rest of the poem.

"I went to bed thinking about the Pashtun word," on the other hand, is more intriguing as a beginning; the poem is off and running. (Though I am not entirely convinced by this casual declaration. Does the writer really know some Pashtun, that he or she can mull over its ironies, or is this just a "factoid" picked up somewhere?) Lines 4 through 16 are the meat of the poem, and there is greater momentum, but we still run across occasional flat language. The moon looks "sublime." Hmmm. On the other hand, there is also some skilled word- and sound-play: "unfazed" (unphased?), "red-eye"/"eye level"/"leveling." The couplet, while lovely in its own right, didn't quite work for me—it had that tacked-on feel that so many sonnet couplets have (including many of Shakespeare's).

I do like the voice, the conversational quality that moves easily from foreign words to newspaper gossip to a transatlantic flight. Perhaps the poet relies too much on the title and repeating moon image to connect the wife-beating, remarriage, and soul-searching. The poet has something interesting to say here. Why not say it?

•

Few titles work as well with their poems as this one does: the ever-shifting series of images/ideas that the narrator plays with rapidly become a conduit for our understanding of the narrator's emotional state. The poem is electric in its jumps between images, river-like in its psychological meanderings. I am fascinated that I assumed the speaker was female, an assumption challenged beautifully by the above respondent. This changes my reading significantly, since the poem is charged with physical or sexual menace due to the "man-with-no-penis"/"man-who-doesn't-beat-his-wife" lines that raise deeper questions as to why *this* narrator needs to "level" with him/herself. If the speaker is female, the menace is largely from outside and most likely in the past, though there are clear self-doubts she has for engaging in any relationship in which she was a victim. I suppose it is largely solipsism that makes me believe the narrator is female, but the moon is traditionally a feminine symbol, and this image of the (potential) self staring back at the self, seeing the self "eye to eye" in fact, makes such a connection possible, if unlikely. There is also an eerie distance created in the poem with that repetition of "level"/"leveling," the vague use of "our" and "us," and the image of the woman whose remarriage is featured in the *Times*.

With all the quick turns this poem takes, it's as if the narrator is too afraid (or too numb) to see the truth of herself and her marriage except through anecdotes about people only distantly seen or related: to an extent, the speaker becomes the moon gazing back at her own life. For a while I even played with the idea that the woman in the *Times* article was in fact the speaker, but ultimately I didn't buy it.

If the narrator is a man, however—which seems more likely—the menace isn't external but internal, and the distancing elements of the poem take on a greater weight for me as reader (if it's a female speaker, the poem feels more like avoiding surface). It certainly explains the nervous, jumpy feel to the images. There is one part of the poem that disturbs me if the speaker is male, however, and it's that last couple of lines in which the speaker declares that he wants his nerve, not his naïveté back. What specifically does he mean by naïveté? We do see that nerve, in this poem, has been equated—if comically or anthropologically—with the ability to fight back when one's authority is being challenged, especially by a woman. The moon's "indifferent" gaze and "implacable" waves then could seem threatening to this male speaker even as the moon forces him to be honest with himself, hence possibly changing the tone of the poem from self-revelation to an embittered plea for forgiveness. "Implacable" is an especially interesting word, since it suggests that nothing the speaker does will ever please his judge—a charge not uncommon among those who physically abuse their spouses. This is, admittedly, carrying the point of the poem *way* too far, but this is work that relies heavily on changes of tone and the nuance of repetition rather than explicit details, so questions of the narrator's sexual identity and his/her relation to the menace and despair implicit in this poem must be expected.

Christopher Merrill

THE FENCE

Once upon a time is what the fence dividing up a mountain range announces, in lines at once irregular and even.

For drama it depends upon a clear beginning, middle, and end. Its effects? Cathartic, purging landowners of their terror, interlopers of their pity. *On guard!* the playwright cries. *All the world's a fence*, the groundlings say.

In the ancient quarrel between fancy and the imagination the fence takes both sides. Nor does it distinguish between form and content, poetry and prose.

These are the four directions of the fence: up, down, right, wrong, black, white, male, female. Nevertheless, at night the fence points only toward the future, time's true north.

In Tennessee someone is pouring the wilderness into a jar—that's one way to build a fence. Here's another: trace a pebble's lineage back to Creation.

Vested with moonflowers and intimations of the miraculous, the fence tilts into the hills, loosening its nails in a provocative fashion, unbuckling the armor men are saving for the final days.

See how the fence swaggers in the wind, embodying a
dying sense of justice; how it casts a shadow over the
rumpled sheets of mud tucked into an arroyo in the
wake of a flash flood; how it reveals our weakness
for design.

For we carried the fence, like our accents and dances,
into the wilds of this sprawling continent, where it
survived our twangs and replaced our two-steps.

This is where we sang until our throats—our thoughts—
were raw. And this is what results from myth giving
way to law and history. Who will accept the fence's
first, and final, offer?

The earth itself is a fence, according to the cartographers
of the afterlife, in a universe awash in fences—a belief
the demographers reject. Obscured by the rivers and
rock walls the fence crosses and climbs is one stark
fact: whether the world ends in fire or ice, the fence
will live happily ever after.

•

I enjoy poems about poems about the process of writing poems
about 50 percent of the time I see them. Fortunately, "The Fence"
falls on that side which impresses the senses of mind, body, and
soul. I am brought back to Stevens's jar in Tennessee, to Keats's
Grecian urn, and Poe's raven. This fence does not separate body
and soul, intellect and sinew, nature and man. This fence unites
everything in its sheer beauty.

•

Again with this poem I as a reader had to experience a slow process of familiarization with the poem before I was able to accept it on its own terms. At first I disliked it: the relatively "abstract" grounding of the poem seemed to provide a glaring, artificial stage for the breezily confident declarative voice. The sometimes inexplicable imagery seemed precious. It seemed as if the ethos embodied and enacted in the poem was less than serious. As I continued to read the poem, I simply got used to it, although I suppose I could say that I began to understand it. The fence symbolizes something complex, unnameable: culture? human knowledge? art? the mind's inevitable divisiveness? all of the above? The poem creates the image in a series of exciting, dramatic voice-gestures without reducing it to explanation. Although the rhetorical design of the poem is a little too faux French for me, I respect its intelligence and integrity.

•

I immediately liked this poem, returning to it again and again over the course of a few days as I considered what I might say that would explain (increase?) its value to me as a reader. The poem to me speaks elegantly of borders—sexual, geographic, racial, artistic—that we establish as ways to organize the world. Whether arbitrary or natural, we're attracted to "fences," and I loved the delightful little shocks of recognition I got from lines like: "These are the four directions of the fence: up, down, right, wrong, black, white, male, female" (I might have mixed up the "directions" a bit, so that "female" doesn't occur in the same rhythmic balance as "wrong") and "[f]or we carried the fence, like our accents and dances, into the wilds of this sprawling continent." The only gestures this poem makes that I don't trust as a writer are the lines that make the fence too abstract: the fence "embod[ies] a dying sense of justice"? Its effects are "[c]athartic, purging landowners of their terror, interlopers of their pity"?

Those lines are the hardest to imagine certainly, and distract from the real intelligence and beauty displayed by the rest of the poem.

•

A playfulness runs through "The Fence"—from the fairy-tale formula of its beginning and end to its allusions/appropriations, made sometimes with a light touch, sometimes bold-faced—not that the poet is trying to hide anything or, I think, show off. Instead, its allusions feel metaphorical, like a game of dress-up with clothes from a child's dress-up box, a game which, as anyone who has seen children in action knows, is serious though—wearing those oversized shoes, sometimes clomping—play. Not that this is a clumsy piece: it is polished, quizzical, quixotic. I like the way the doubled "four" directions veer off in their own direction and I find beauty in the shadow cast "over the rumpled sheets of mud" and especially in "This is where we sang until our throats—our thoughts—were raw." What a nice conjunction, throats and thoughts. I'm also much moved by the final serious thought—"The earth itself is a fence, according to the cartographers of the afterlife. . . ." Playful and thought-provoking, this piece demarcates its terrain in surprising, imaginative ways.

•

Good fences make good neighbors; good poems make me happy. I like the verve and playfulness of this, the lack of irony, the inclusive reach of its allusions and diction (able to contain easily both Aristotle and two-steps), its shameless puns ("On guard!"), the precision of language ("Vested with moonflowers"), its sweep (from real arroyos to the geography of the Underworld). The stretched-out lines themselves seem at once to fence and stretch the page; nor does the poem distinguish "between form and content, poetry and prose." This is a poem that takes "both sides."

I particularly like how it takes what might well be negative (fences, boundaries, limits) and makes it positive. (It is also refreshing to read a poem in praise of boundaries that is so unabashedly free verse; this is usually the metier of sonnets.) It wears its ars poetica lightly but all the more effectively for that. On a first read, I had some reservations about some of the balder allusions (the Tennessee jar, fire and ice), but the swagger of "The Fence" won me over. How can I quibble? It is a treat to read a poem without low ceilings.

•

In terms of meaning and conceit, this poem is brilliant!—I don't say that lightly. The body, creation, race, politics, so much else—each discursive imagining of the barrier, the "fence" is fully realized, and though this is a long poem, my attention never wandered. I kept asking: "What next?! Boy, this is a serious fence!" The structure of the poem also breaks that "fence," since the wraparound stanzas mimic historic prose, but there is enough of some really good rhythm to drive the poem forward, to separate from "just" prose. A true prose poem—I still haven't figured out how to write one myself.

•

Long Island is a universe awash in "invisible" fences. I visited my mother out near Stony Brook last week, and heard the story of how Jose, her tan Chihuahua, had received a shock from one one day—not physically, but psychically.

This is the problem with the invisible. My mother spent a fortune she didn't have on her "invisible" fence but now will never force the corresponding collar on Jose because it's too cruel. Obviously, this is the same problem with the invisible, but looked at too subjectively.

Poor Jose must have thought his inability to cross that boundary was all his fancy!

Gloria Vando

CANTE JONDO

Segovia says Lorca was killed
by a jealous lover, but I know
that isn't so, I know he was seized
from midnight reverie, pried screaming
from the poem in his head, the lover
beside him pleading with Franco's men
before the butt end of a German carbine
careened him into a wordless sleep
taking him worlds away from Lorca
Guernica and the caves of Andalucia
from the fifth column, the Falange, death
far, far from death, deep into a dream
sweetened by seas, seeping slowly
into Moroccan fields where boys
culipandeando ignite the lighteyed
lust of tourists who come down
to excavate their scraggy yield—
Arabs preferring the ripe, moist meat
of melons—and Lorca's lover lying
in that crazy hardon dream, oblivious
of what was going on, unconscious
of his own demise—with the poet gone
who would immortalize his soul?—and
the barrel of a rifle prodding Lorca's
chest like the insistent finger of Uncle
Sam, hard up against his anus, prying

open his mouth *muévelo, maricón* and
Lorca's face green as the craters
of his vellum moon, his body twisted,
a hibiscus against the dawn, stumbles
ahhh! as they jab him on, blindfold
filth across his eyes, *those eyes,* bind
laces from his shoes into his wrists so
when he staggers to the wall his shoes
drag through the gravel, unravelling
the earth's tears, the earth's dark song

drrrggge drrrggge dirige
Domine Deus meus in conspectu tuo...

Lorca, my poet, shot down in prayer,
while his lover unaware sleeps and dreams
of almond eyes and bougainvillea.
Homosexuals die violent deaths, Segovia
says, playing a Bach fugue on his guitar.

NOTES:

culipandeando: swaying hips (coined by poet Palés Matos);

muévelo: move it;

maricón: derogatory term for homosexual;

dirige. . . : direct O Lord my God, my way in thy sight.

•

"Cante Jondo" conjures a dream state where violence and love
intermingle in language's passion, where the intensities of
opposite emotions blur and overlap as in a dream state, and tone

is more vital than hue, pushing the poem deep and insistently into the visceral glories of indignity and pain, death, deep into a dream, seas, seeping slowly, green as the craters of his vellum moon, his body twisted, a hibiscus against the dawn, ending with a Bach fugue, the blind acuity of art.

·

"Cante Jondo" is an example of the best kind of collaboration—the spirit of one poet inhabiting another, beyond pastiche, homage, or elegy. Cascading down enjambed lines, "Cante Jondo" echoes Lorca's cadences and revels in his inclusivity but also displays original features, "immortalizing" a lover whom Lorca's own poems do not celebrate. While contrasting surrealism with classicism, "Cante Jondo" also employs fugue-like elements—counterpointing the murder against the dream: Lorca's eyes are blinded with filth while the lover "dreams of almond eyes and bougainvillea." The unconscious has provided material for much surrealist poetry; here it is structured, framed, and given an explicitly political dimension by the rhetorical assertion of the first lines, "Segovia says Lorca was killed / by a jealous lover, but I know / that isn't so" and by the poem's savagely poignant and ironic final chord.

·

This is a vivid poem that turns the specific case of one man's murder into a representative one, making a political statement about violence against homosexuals. Why was Lorca murdered by Falangists? Because his politics were misread? Because he was gay? Either is possible, I suppose, though I am not aware that we have conclusive evidence. This author has decided that Lorca was a martyr to sexuality, it would seem, and I honestly do not know whether or not the evidence agrees.

The poem is full of passionate conflations, and while seeing room for agreement, I wonder if they are entirely accurate and just. Is "the insistent finger of Uncle / Sam" a way of pairing this injustice with those perpetrated in our own country? If so, is that accurate? Obviously, gays have been murdered—I think immediately of Matthew Shepard—but is there a kind of unhelpful generalization implied by this simile? And what of Segovia? What exactly is the case about him? What is he accused of, playing apparently dispassionate German music at the closing of this passionate poem? Is this a kind of Romantic denunciation? If so, I find its politics suspect while at the same time feeling sympathy for its subject, poor Lorca, who wrote so beautifully.

•

Lorca published *Poema del Cante Jondo* (literally, "deep song") in 1921, its Andalusian *saetas*, the editors note in their Preface to the 1955 *Selected Poems*, typically "sung without guitar accompaniment while the images of Christ and the Virgin pass by in the Holy Week processions." This contemporary "Cante Jondo" approximates song in its internal rhyming, willful assonance, insistent alliteration ("from the fifth column, the Falange, death / far, far from death, deep into a dream / sweetened by seas, seeping slowly"), and in its headlong rush, its charged, vertical thrust that trusts the associative imagery of its run-on sentences to convey its urgency. The adolescent surety of its knowledge ("I know / . . . I know") and its worshipful stance ("into his wrists" and the Latin prayer both intimating the crucified Christ) are less convincing, finally, than its touching interjectional phrase ("those eyes") that catches in the poem's throat and humanizes its political indignation. Less concerned with history itself (Guernica was bombed in 1937, the year *after* Lorca's execution) than with its muted reverberations, less memorable for diction than for an affective narration, less dependent upon logic than upon its own "crazy hardon dream," this poem succeeds on its own terms, evoking Lorca, aptly, through a passionate, homoerotic Catholicism.

•

Passionate as it is, this poem is so haphazardly written, so far, that I lose interest in it after a reading or three. I say "so far" because surely the poet will give himself to his poem again until line divisions become consistently necessary and add complex power, until its dozen or more extra words are excised (so that the poem finds its meaningful music), until those indulgences and lurches common to first drafts give way to one inevitable rhythm of feeling that renders the reader's reservations mute. Even the wildest poems of dream/displacement/rave/rapture/ terror/unraveling anger and grief must reach coherence as, so far, the promising "Cante Jondo" does not.

•

Reading this poet—or her/his persona—claim Lorca as her/his poet is, for me, like seeing Bill Clinton don a Tupac T-shirt: I admire the spirit but I have to turn away, embarrassed for us all. While there's fine, exciting language throughout (and many other successes)—rightly praised by other reviewers—I find the poem at once pretentious, sentimental, and superficially political. These are heavy—no doubt hyperbolic—charges that I bring, with irony and goodwill and no small amount of self-doubt, into the spirit of this book, but I think they're worth examining.

First, Segovia, the great Spanish guitarist, the "father of classical guitar," seems to be used here as the artist reactionary against whom Lorca sang his songs; while I don't know anything of Segovia's politics, I do know that Segovia—single-handedly, it seems—made his traditionally lower-class instrument respectable, made the tradition bend to him, popularized the instrument, and therefore helped set the stage for the guitar's central place in the working-class revolution of rock—a revolution, I suspect, that Lorca would have supported with all his heart.

Second, could this poem be more premeditated, more un-Lorca-like? Could a Persian pony dance on the moonlit plaza of a forehead here? No.

Third and finally, Lorca actually lived; he didn't continuously pray or write poems; he is a martyr, if he is one, to life, to our shared legacy of intolerance and hatred. That's why his poems will continue to move us: he captured something of the fugitive nature of our desires and their disappointments. That he was gay, leftist, whatever; these are sentimental, simple ways to explain what Lorca himself would not; his poems provide stunning, unanswerable questions; this one provides a salve—however finely blended—to hide that wound.

David Daniel

THE WORD

As brutally as bees drive their tongues to flower,
As gentle as that seems to us,
So let us live our ordinary dying,
This morning glory, this fiery star gone nod:
Here's the pure tongue of words becoming
As they also pass away: Listen, then kiss me:
The last sound we'll hear will be the silence
Of our first word finally formed, our first sweet and
    violent tasting.

•

My first response to this poem was to dismiss it. Its brevity and its unencumbered discursiveness sounded at first like facility. I heard echoes of that preachy Rilkean tone, that sequined drag-queen gown that so many American poets, probably embarrassed by the suburban mediocrity of the English they hear, adore wearing. I felt somewhat uncomfortable with the first line, "As brutally as bees drive their tongues to flower"; the "brutally" seeming excessive, "editorial." But eventually I began to hear the poem on its own terms a little more clearly, and came to like it more. I slowly appreciated the integrity of its thoughtfulness. The linearity of the argument, stretched across a long, multiclaused sentence, began to seem the result of engaged thinking. The nuances of the imagery and tone (the eroticism of bees, the ambiguity of that first line, even the disembodied character of the voice) were all finally justified in my imagination, and I learned to find the poem beautiful.

In and of itself, it still seems fragmentary to me. This isn't necessarily a bad thing . . . like everyone else, I love all those tiny poems in translation that one can memorize while stuck trying to make a left-hand turn against heavy traffic. I'm sure that "The Word" was once thirty or forty lines longer than it is now and that a lot of hard thinking went into its compression. The poem seems fragmentary simply because aspects of its approach to its theme are still questionable. How seriously does this poet take the issue of violence? In this poet's work, is "pretty" language pretentious or is it a tonal medium that seems "won"? And, finally, is this a boy or a girl? Because I'm being asked to kiss the poet, I think I have a right to know that.

·

What I loved about the poem first was its sound, so it took me a moment really to dig out meaning. Once I started that, however, I too was brought up short by that first line. The bee "brutally" digging its tongue into the flower made me think of cunnilingus—and made the line unintentionally both vicious and comic, since the bee is a tiny creature and almost any flower (or woman's sex organ) would certainly engulf it.

I'm taking a moment to reflect on how grotesque I'm making this sound.

The following lines I don't believe, and it largely has to do with the adverb "brutally" in the first image: Why is this act now suddenly "gentle"? What is that "ordinary dying"? If we continue with the sexual connotations of the poem, then this perhaps becomes orgasm, which in turn is compared to the impermanence of speech. I have a bias against poems about language, and this lyric of verbal and sexual impermanence ("the pure tongue of words becoming / As they also pass away") is something that may be too romantic for me. That said, however, I think the poem's very old-fashionedness in music and idea is what makes it refreshing. But ultimately I'm not convinced by this poem's paradoxes: brutal/gentle, sweet/violent, sound/ silence. This, however, is my fault; because I won't mourn the transience of words and because I don't care about the inherent impermanence of desire, I'm not anxious about the paradoxes these subjects represent.

One last thing: the first respondent wondered about the poet's sex. Though I don't agree that it's relevant, I would (as a woman) assume this speaker is male. The floral imagery here seems solely female, and this poet doesn't appear interested in inverting poetic stereotypes. There is also something *very* distantly Marvell about that last injunction for the reader to kiss the poet just after the poet has mourned the "pass[ing] away" of "the pure tongue." All beauty's fleeting, even yours. Get it while you can.

•

On the whole, I enjoy this poem, logos as (pro)creation. Might the poem be more mysterious if you cut "then kiss me"? One other quibble: do bees have tongues? Forgoing personification, perhaps the poem could open with "As brutally as we drive our tongues to flower." These suggestions would neutralize the issue of the gender of the speaker raised by the other respondents.

•

This poem is keenly aware of transience: the moment of becoming is also the moment of passing away. And with that recognition there's the familiar carpe diem theme: "then kiss me." What makes this poem distinctive, however, is the attention to sound, silence, and language. It's "Listen, then kiss me"; it's "the pure tongue of words"; it's the paradox of "the last sound we hear will be the silence" that twists and renews this perennial theme in a contemporary way.

Yet, despite its careful craft—the poem is, with many twists, linguistically one sentence—I wish the poem engaged me more. I'm unconvinced by the second line, "As gentle as that seems to us." Because the argument of the poem has the form of a, b, so c, I need to experience the first two assertions as undeniably vivid and true. Instead, the second line leaves me questioning its veracity, and I doubt the ensuing motion of the poem. Maybe if there was more development to the poem, I would feel the lovely assertion of the last two lines has been earned.

•

General, abstract, and almost vague on its surface, this poem opens up eventually to the reading tongue like the flower it describes, like the moment it embodies. The tone is quiet, the syntax simple, the metrics conventional, yet the poem takes in its stride strangenesses: "star gone nod," two colons in a row, great rhythmic variation. The strategies seem there not for their own sake but in the service of a communication that could have been conveyed no other way. I trust the insight of the vision that can guide this poem so surely through these various strategies. This poem does not have the most accessible surface, but once that surface is entered through slow rereading, the poem rewards my attention with the profound union of word and effect that is the aim of the art.

•

So much in this poem seems to depend upon accepting the assumptions of the speaker. The poem is declarative and begins with the argument "as brutally as bees," "as gentle as that seems," *so* "let us live our ordinary dying." I found myself only partially able to accept this, perhaps because, being too much of a biological mind, I do not see how "bees drive their tongues to flower," and so from the beginning feel that the language is personified. These seem less real bees than bees as a metaphor for human feeling. The reader is much directed here, "Here's the pure tongue" "Listen, then kiss me"; and this along with the declarative statements, as if merely stating what is, makes me wonder what is at risk here? Only "The Word" the poem tells me, and yet the assumptions suggest much more that I am not invited into, and so, while I feel the direction to which I am being directed, I cannot finally believe or assent to the kiss which the poem means to be.

Rachel Blau DuPlessis

DRAFT 31: SERVING WRIT

Given
>>that the work undertaken to date
>>>>glosses two words: IT and IS
>and sets nomads a-wander
>>thru and fro this site
>>>>graven with rivulets of marking;
Given
>>that "the common air includes
>>>>Events listening to their own tremors,"
>them in "unassuaged unrest" at the prospect
>>of "adding another edge to the page"—
>>>>even a hairline crack
>articulated from seepage and stipple
>>"disquieting in its shadow
>>>>and its rage";
Given
>>its joy; right, given Joy:
>>>>Go flash pink swells
>Go "gold sweat" high and blinding
>>where crows work over the last at last,
>>>>eh-eh-eh-eh ah ah eh-eh-eh-eh
>exacting number codes of 2 and 4
>>they do, and lurk over the lintels of every door
>>>>that opens on the filiated Here,

Beech, Dog, Loggia, Pitcher, Vertigo
      thereby Hear—every unspeakable untellable
           X, its pluck and jube,
                its incalculable harmonics toll.

Given all this, there is nothing but this to say.
      The work has exceeded its original memory.

October-November 1996

NOTES:

"common air . . . ," Zukofsky, A-6;

"another edge . . . ," Rod Smith;

"disquieting . . . ," Luce Irigaray;

"gold sweat," Barbara Guest.

•

The third stanza of "Draft 31: Serving Writ" is a culmination of Romantic tendencies in the earlier stanzas, tendencies that counter well the logical and syntactic imperatives of "Given," "Go," and "thereby Hear." Because of the passions of phrasing and image in these middle lines—lines such as "Go flash pink swells," "and lurk over the lintels of every door" that opens to "the filiated Here, / Beech, Dog, Loggia, Pitcher, Vertigo," and "its pluck and jube"—one hears beneath any didacticism the pleasures of emotional response, even to single words. Yes, of course the poet is a smart person, and we can admire the distancing that is achieved by reference to other poets in "Notes" and the high tonal ranges that surely remind us of Gerard Manley Hopkins in references to number and code and also in some of the diction—glosses, articulated, exacting. (The poet wants to comment on emotion, it would appear, so that the feeling isn't soupy or slack.) But the harmonics of the poem include "Joy," and ultimately the poem is less about intelligence than Wordsworth's "overflow." Further, the poem makes sense—not that a benign obscurity is a bad thing when one can do no better for a complexity or passion sweeps through. I wonder if my favor for the poem is in part based on my belief that art surely can exceed "its original memory," as the poet says in the final line—memory I take as being involved both with the past ("recollected in tranquility") and with imagination. Who of us in our judgments is inured to belief? Still, I am pleased to read the poem several times not so much for restatement of my ideas but because of the passionate syntax and the beauty of some phrasings.

•

As a poem about the rift and longing between intuited, perhaps illusory presence (the sense suggested by the words "it" and "is") and the language that would gesture toward that presence, which would in so doing "serve" it, this poem manages neither to succumb to a facility of meaningless fracture nor to lapse into despair over the sense of alienation implied by the failure of signs to contain stable essences. Nor does the poem opt for an easy irony that fails to honor or commit. The poem is one of praise and gratitude. While suggesting some familiar insights about the instability of language (appearing here in "rivulets" and haunted by what it lacks, what lies outside the edge of the page), the poem works toward a surprising sense of surplus and joy, of remarkable and unlikely abundance associated with the music (and in turn, the wonder) of the unspeakable. As a poem about service, it is likewise a poem about bestowal. Hence we have the chorusing of the word "given" and the texture of given texts recalled by the poem, recast in a renewing context. What is given is in part "original memory" (a phrase that echoes the desire for first things, for original presence, but that suggests as well the sense of all things as mediated, as tainted by a sense of what's remembered, what's lost). What is given in turn is the aesthetic experience of language driven by desire, transfigured into song, exceeding the experience of loss. In such a world, language "tolls" in elegy, in praise.

•

As early as in its title this poem announces that its subject is language itself. Our next clues are the clash of officialese ("the work undertaken to date") with self-conscious poesy ("nomads a-wander") and an occasional attractive consonance ("graven with rivulets"). Such juxtapositions warn me that I'm in by-now familiar terrain and that the poem means to dismiss as irrelevant or misguided my appetite for meaning—perhaps by bombarding me with empty phrases in imitation of the media-saturated world through which I walk daily.

Soon, though, the poem's wordplay is complicated by the phrase "the common air includes / Events listening to their own tremors." So silence, too, is the subject here. In making its reader aware of the echoes and spaces between the words, the poem wants to add "another edge to the page." That these, the poem's most interesting moments, come from other sources feels for a moment like a kind of intellectual name-dropping. Still, heartened, I press on, wondering how to connect the ecstatic language of "Go flash pink swells" and "'gold sweat' high and blinding" with what follows, the abstraction of the crows' cacklings to "number codes." The mismatched dictions and random images remind me of channel-surfing, of the restless drive to consume that can keep me clicking from one incomplete thought to the next until my eyes glaze over and I'm too exhausted to walk away. Is this what I want from a poem, I wonder? No—but yes, in the sense that a good poem should give some kind of sense of what it's like to be alive at this moment in history. And if I want more, a little epiphany or at least a slightly transformed understanding of the world, the poem at its end at least nudges me toward stasis: "The work has exceeded its original memory." It knows what I want from it: to resonate beyond its ending, to know more than I do, more than its author intends. It fully understands the desires it declines to fulfill.

•

Poems, like this one, in the so-called "L=A=N=G=U=A=G=E poetry" mode, give my students—and many of my contemporaries—fits and evoke from them reactions that are in fact reactionary, which is a shame, if an understandable one, since more than 90 percent of such poems are smug, self-indulgent crap designed to provoke such reactions. Of course, the unpleasant—and often unspoken—historical truth is that more than 90 percent of all poems written at any given time in any mode—like, say, poems in the so-called "workshop mode"—are subject to similar charges: they just aren't very good, despite their intelligence, goodwill, intense feeling, and so on. Most obviously the trouble begins for my students, at least, because these so-called "L=A=N=G=U=A=G=E poems" often lack the overt subject matter that allows an easily articulated response; that is, there's no epiphanic moment in a grandmother's attic, no particularly lovely observation or painful heartbreak, so the reader's left adrift in the language and forced to pass judgment, which in our age is, by virtue of its elitist scent, nearly taboo. Some people are better at writing poems than others, and their work tends to transcend the categories of "language poetry," "workshop poetry," "beat poetry," "formalist poetry," or whatever. These are difficult things to discuss: What is good taste? What—if anything—does subject matter have to do with it? Why do we tend to value Celan over Sachs, Frost over Edward Thomas, any poet over his or her contemporary writing about essentially the same subjects in essentially the same manner?

"Draft 31: Serving Writ" is a good poem, and I'll try to say briefly why I think so—and why too the poem comes up a little short of greatness. First, the range of its diction is extraordinarily broad and brings to mind Crane, who might well have written "incalculable harmonics toll." I could choose almost anything as an example: from the Anglo-Saxon *writ* ("document," plus the legal notion of ordering or prohibiting some action, and the introduction of the legal trope of the entire poem) to the Latinate *gloss* (from "tongue" and "glow") to such stunning usages—such wonderful play—as "filiated Here" and "pluck and jube," the poem presents a cornucopia of fresh language from which to, well, pluck—then taste. Finding such treasure recalls for me the deepest, most inspiring joys of a life in poetry; this fact alone separates "Draft 31" from the great majority of contemporary poems in any mode.

And of course, even if it takes a moment to discover, there *is* a subject: the poem's composition, its own struggle to *be*—in this way it is akin at bottom to the most significant lyric poems from Sappho to Keats to Celan to whomever. But most of those other poems have some other subject matter floating at the surface—even if it's as simple as Hopkins's hardened heart being stirred one morning by a bird—which acts as an excuse, one might say, to explore that other, deeper matter. That "excuse" is not a trivial one but rather—calling up the word's roots—provides a "pardon from the charge"—an impossible one—to capture the experience of the world in language while asserting the necessity of trying to nonetheless: we are charged even if we must fail. The "excuse"—that bird flying overhead or whatever—helps reveal the tragic significance of our daily failure to articulate much of anything meaningfully—the underlying elegy that is the song of our lives and of all great lyric poetry. For me, while stimulating, beautiful, and absolutely masterful, "Draft 31: Serving Writ," lacking that worldly engagement, only recalls those joys above—an extraordinary achievement for which I'm thankful—but it does not enact them anew.

•

So much has been said about this poem (and so well). (Bruce Wexler, who wrote, "Poetry Is Dead. Does Anybody Care?" in his *Newsweek* May 5, 2003 article on the unimportance of poetry, should see the dust this poem kicks up, or the wake it leaves, rather.) "Draft 31" also serves Wit and the promise of the unexpected. The intention goes *bravado*: "Go flash pink swells / Go 'gold sweat' . . . / eh-eh-eh-eh ah ah . . ." whisking as a pontoon. Given that big wave the slalomed reader must cross, zigzagging behind the boat. Yeats on a ski. A life on the beach. Don't they name their surfboard? Beech, Dog, Loggia, Pitcher, Vertigo? These are Beachers emblazoned with riffs. The poem shakes for itself. But does it? Under the formal Given riding the rivulets of markings, the lines, there is the wave-like repetition of the Given over the play of language. Maybe "Draft 32" will be without the last two lines.

•

I don't know whether to be more perplexed by the poem or by some of the comments. I feel like Alice listening to Humpty Dumpty. What is the well-read but not theory-marinated reader to make of this? One scholiast asserts: "Further, the poem makes sense." Does it? (Earlier the same person says: "The poet wants to comment on emotion, it would appear"; this seems less confident.) Is the tonal range reminiscent of Gerard Manley Hopkins or is it just the pied beauty of "seepage and stipple"? I suppose we can assume from the helpful clue of the title that this is "about" writing/language/revision. What then? Is this a code to be broken by, say, tracking down references? Or a joyride of syllables? (In which case I'd like more unalloyed enjoyment.)

I'm not saying there is nothing to like here. The borrowed phrases are interesting. I like the musical quality of the occasional rhymes, the textures of the diction. The last line makes for a good ending. Then there is the sort of overheated Elizabethansonnet rhetoric (and structure, three "givens" and a couplet), which nods to tradition. There is much that irritates as well, namely that it takes itself so seriously (more notes per line than "The Wasteland"). But doesn't this fall into the category of nonsense verse—that is, it more or less retains the grammar and syntax of English—though I have reservations about "thru and fro" and, in stanza two, "them"—while evading pin-down-able traditional "sense"? I am an admirer of true nonsense verse, from Lear and Carroll through much of Ashbery. But is something deep just because we don't get it? Though maybe I'm the only one who doesn't!

Michael Waters

MISERERE

We're bathing together when Alina kneels in
    steam
to reveal crimped flaps of skin,
drawn shades the surgeons have fashioned: system
    of pulleys
worked by little metal wheels
screwed into each shoulder. She rolls them with a
    finger:
the shades scroll: I gaze through her,
through windows opened in her chest, past icy
    tendrils
scrawling abandoned gardens
where seven unborn sisters, hands joined in a
    circle,
attempt to sing a sacred
cycle by Górecki or Pärt, a healing chorale
that resurrects starved finches,
lifts fallen fruit back to black branches, replen-
    ishes
green in winter-scorched grasses.
Their voices swell through each scar-rimmed oval.
    O, she says,
look: they've taken both my breasts.
Yes, I reply, but listen: hasn't God replaced them
with such glorious music.

•

This poem seeks to transform the disgrace brought upon Alina, a woman who has survived a double mastectomy. The first five lines attempt to describe what Alina's chest actually looks like—but fail to. As a reader, I cannot discern how her "crimped flaps of skin" are supposed to function as "shades" attached to a "system of pulleys / worked by little metal wheels / screwed into each shoulder." Once these fleshy curtains are lifted, the speaker is able to catch a vision "through windows opened in her chest" of "seven unborn sisters" who "attempt to sing a sacred / cycle by Górecki or Pärt." This seems precious, especially when the speaker reassures Alina that though her breasts are gone, they have been replaced by a "glorious music." This need for personal redemption via art is a typical ambition found in American poetry but, alas, an easy trope. More compelling a rendition on a similar topic would be Robert Hass's prose poem "A Story About the Body" from *Human Wishes*. There we can experience a poem that leaves the wounds open.

•

This poem calls on the reader to play music rather than producing a verbal music of its own. It turns the specific case of a woman who has suffered a double mastectomy into the speaker's fantasy of transcendence through art, but there's too little art in the poem itself. For one thing, its literal statements don't work. How is it that the speaker and Alina have been bathing together but only now, when Alina kneels, are her scars revealed? Who are the seven unborn sisters singing in a circle like critters in Dr. Seuss? Are we supposed to infer some connection to the Pleiades? The seven sorrows of Mary? Why unborn? And why compare the loss of this woman to the historical catastrophes memorialized in music by Górecki and Pärt?

•

Faced with a loss, a bodily violation, so horrible to contemplate, ordinary empathy fails and the speaker disassociates from her normal thinking processes into surrealism. In a bizarre, forced, Frida Kahlo–like series of images, the crimped skin becomes like window shades and the speaker's imagination moves to fantasizing pulleys to open the shades. Completely leaving the original vehicle of the metaphor behind, the speaker allows the fantasy windows to open and another fantasy of a healing chorale to occur. This sequence of images is a daring attempt to represent not Alina's chest but the subjective experience of confronting something one's mind is unable to grasp. In showing the inadequacy of ordinary images to render such experience, the poem paradoxically communicates, through its bizarre and uncommon imagery, a fairly common experience, that of being overwhelmed.

•

To paraphrase badly North America's greatest surrealist, Wallace Stevens, "One has to have a mind of winter." To fully understand this wonderful poem, one must have a mind of mercy. *Miserere* is the first word in the Vulgate text of Psalm 51. Roughly translated, the first stanza goes: "Have mercy on me, O God, according to thy great mercy. And according to the multitude of thy tender mercies blot out my iniquity. Wash me yet more from my iniquity, and cleanse me from my sin." That the poem opens while taking a bath is understandable after reading this psalm. In the last stanza of the psalm, the word "build" shows up. The Hebrew word for "build" means not only "to rebuild" but "to complete what is being built." The music mentioned is by Górecki, but I am sure the poet would also have heard of the choral piece by Gregorio Allegri (1638) which has an early solo section sung by a castrato (male youth whose testes have been removed so he can keep singing high notes). With these sophisticated references, one could thoroughly enjoy this poem and understand its deeper meanings.

•

This is an intriguing, if imperfect, poem. Its alternating lines of thirteen and seven syllables could well signal the poem's dual themes of suffering and salvation. The form the patient/victim's suffering takes is mutilation, whether by legitimate surgeons performing a radical mastectomy to save her life or by rogue surgeons carrying out medical experiments on women during the Holocaust. Here, however, we have salvation: Alina is genuflecting when the seven unborn sisters, in a *voix celeste*, plead with God to resurrect the barren landscape of her torso. They sing, and God responds: The charred effects of radiation from medicine or bombs ("starved finches," "fallen fruit," "black branches," "winter-scorched grasses") vanish as "glorious" sacred music fills each "scar-rimmed" cavity. But though we are invited to look beyond the tangible, to perceive Alina's inner self/beauty, the poet has set up a belabored system of tangible details (pulleys, wheels, screws) that inhibits us from moving forward with grace.

•

I do think "Miserere" is overwhelmed by the mechanisms of its initial conceit, to the detriment of its redemptive vision, and that its redemptive vision is too forced, too pat. There are also two small moments, or movements, which are emblematic to me of a lack of clarity which weakens the poem. Kneeling (see dictionary) is normally associated with moving downward to one's knees—here, Alina *must* be rising from the steam (otherwise her chest would have already been exposed). A small misstep, but one that has the reader confused and compensating from the outset, before even encountering the confusion of the pulleys and so on. Later I wonder why the sisters are made to "attempt to sing" rather than singing: "attempt" signals some difficulty or inability, perhaps an interesting difficulty overcome, but as it is left unexplored, "attempt" is out of place with the miraculous healing powers attributed to the "glorious music."

This poem does move me where its imagery is simplest and strains least. "Crimped flaps of skin" and "I gaze . . . / through windows opened in her chest, past icy tendrils / scrawling abandoned gardens" are good descriptions of the inner and outer desolation the surgery has created. (I wish the sad "starved finches" were part of this initial image and not part of the healing, because I find them, but not their resurrection, convincing.) I am also convinced by the visionary, healing music in one line—"voices swell through each scar-rimmed oval"—which is in itself one of the most lyrical moments in the poem and carries within in it both loss and the possibility of redemption.

Michelle Boisseau

SMITHEREENS

Quick rivulets glide alongside the ice
piled high in the gutter, the windows go

dark, maybe there's a sob. Someone, maybe
someone who's not living yet, takes hold

of the sheet and yanks it over my head.
My loosened clothes removed, I'm wheeled along,

doors open and close. Like the river through town
I'm indifferently touched by many hands.

Snow flops from branches, oaks shrug their leaves,
unconfined, I am no longer confounded

like morning fog. Solids instantly steam
as I'm conveyed into the blank of a sun,

the crematory blaze where I begin
to sing, to wrack and whistle in the fire

that flares my flesh and then my restive bones
as I reform myself in clouds.

•

Even though there is no "I" in this poem until the third stanza, the "I"s this reader hears in "glide" and "ice piled high" clue me in to the fact that this is a very personal poem. The speaker's passive death wish is completely compelling—s/he is "wheeled along" and "conveyed." Not until s/he is burning does s/he "begin / to sing." The economy of this poem is astonishing— and the form holds the content well: the fluidity of the couplets, the enjambment that happens in every stanza except the last in which the speaker "reform[s]." I'm struck by the word "reform"— its religious and spiritual use and also its meaning "to form again," as both seem to be happening in "Smithereens." The poem's title invites chaos while the text reassembles that chaos. I found myself reading it again and again.

•

A death wish? I don't think so. But a poem perched on the fine line between life and death, consciousness and its absence. Obliquely I'm reminded of Emily Dickinson's poem 465, "I heard a Fly buzz—when I died—." This poem invites me back through its precision and mystery, its dashings and reformations. I feel, as I often do with the very best poems, just on the edge of understanding.

•

The run-on sentences and ungainly imagery ("snow flops") give this poem a distinct first-draft quality. Nor is the process particularly illuminating; after all, everyone dies and reenters the physical world. This poem approaches transcendence, but I need more.

•

It is the river through town that struck me. A sudden break from the clutching and the wheeling of the hospital emergency room imagery. I get that the poem is about some sort of transformation or transcendence but not sure to what or for what. I would like to learn more.

•

I'm afraid people are being skimpy because they don't like the poem as much as they like or have liked some of the others, and I'm afraid I agree with those people (if that's indeed how they feel). The structure, the concept, are certainly promising—it's a dream-vision of wintertime death and fiery (sunlike, phoenix-like) rebirth as the speaker moves from the death of water and earth into the life of fire and air. (Stanley Kunitz used to write such poems regularly, as did Louise Bogan.)

The language doesn't do the concept justice. "Quick" is too normal an adjective for "rivulets" and "alongside" seems odd (though not factually wrong) if the ice really does lie in piles (if the piles are "high," "below" would make better sense to me). "Some-one . . . not living yet, takes hold / / of the sheet and yanks it over my head" is finely thought—I love the "yet" (the vision predicts the future rather than replaying the past)—but "maybe" seems oddly casual, too casual in a dream-vision context: Shouldn't the visionary know who it is? If he or she doesn't know, shouldn't it just read "someone" or give a sense-impression ("a figure," "a shape," "a shade")? "Loosened" clothes: By whom? By someone? (By orderlies?) "Removed" is blank (and ambiguous—it sounds at first like an intransitive verb, as if the clothes had removed themselves, or as if the clothes, being English, removed to a superior locale). What rivers are "indifferently touched by many hands"? Lots of people touch the Ganges, but they're far from indifferent; people don't just uncaringly stick their hands in the Hudson, for example, or not en masse. "I am no longer confounded / like morning fog": No longer like confounded fog, or no longer confounded (as fog, under undisclosed circumstances, stops being confounded)? "Solids instantly steam": Solid what? (Solid colors, as opposed to stripes?) Why "instantly" (as against, simply, "Solids steam")? I see attempts at a Hopkins-like straining of language in the second-to-last line, as "flares" becomes weirdly transitive, but the suggestion of flared trousers ruins it for me (and where else does one see "flared" as a transitive verb?); the bones are no longer "restive" if they're applying themselves wholeheartedly to this new and fiery recrudescence, and "reform"—while it might mean, denotatively, what the visionary speaker wants it to mean: "find an entirely new shape for; recrudesce, re-coalesce"— doesn't work connotatively at all, because we normally encounter the word in political contexts (Grover Cleveland reformed the civil service in 1885). The remarkable vision and scenario haven't yet found the words that do it justice—but the best touches here suggest that in the future it might.

•

A hunk a hunk of burning love, I guess, this sweetly mysterious poem. Sorry. I admire the wackiness of the subject—the body being cremated, so commonplace, so strange—and the lyric triumphs along the way: the river, the "wrack and whistle." There's a very interestingly jagged imagination at work here. But I think the poem suffers by its diction; the title, "Smithereens," opens the diction door to allow for almost anything—and it tempts the reader to expect as much, *anything*—but while the imagination wanders to fascinating places, the diction remains (with the fine exception of "yanks") decidedly bound to the lyric-poem homestead, and so the reader's expectations—mine at least—are mostly unfulfilled, and the poem ends, both linguistically and imagistically, very ordinarily.

There is, to me, a lesson that might be learned here that might be phrased this way: diction determines destiny—or at least tries to. While this poem starts out defying lyric convention, it quickly, mostly, gives in to it. And this example—whether applied to narrative, lyrical, formal, beat, or what-have-you poetry—presents a challenge for us all, especially so since this poet is so obviously talented.

Arthur Sze

OX-HEAD DOT

Ox-head dot, wasp waist, mouse tail,
bamboo section, water-caltrop, broken branch,
stork leg, a pole for carrying fuel:
these are the eight defects when a beginning
calligrapher has no bone to a stroke.

I have no names for what can go wrong:
peeling carrots, a woman collapses
when a tumor in her kidney ruptures;
bronze slivers from a gimbal nut
jam the horizontal stabilizer to a jet,

make it plunge into the Pacific Ocean;
"Hyena!" a man shouts into the darkness
and slams shut the door. Stunned, I hear
a scratching, know that I must fumble,
blunder, mistake, fail; yet, sometimes

in the darkest space is a white fleck,
ox-head dot; and when I pass through,
it's a spurt of match into flame,
glowing moths loosed into air, air
rippling, roiling the surface of the world.

•

Sometimes the marvels of language are found in the process of orientation—that is, when I encounter the tumult of modified nouns in the first stanza, I am dizzied. When I begin to tumble into "sense," it is almost a disappointment—I too stumble, blunder, make mistakes in reading. I do enjoy swirling from modern translations of old terms for errors into modern errors of destabilization. I also enjoy being in the presence of a consciousness, an intelligence, within the constraints of this poem, which can range among cultural contexts, if not cultural constants. The pleasures of this poem, however, are also pained and painful.

There is that word, "hyena," shouted in the almost-center of the poem—like "fire" in a crowded theater. Any word will do, it seems to say. Just know enough to be afraid. Every word means danger, every calligraphy is a warning, whether crudely or skillfully rendered hardly matters.

•

A fan of poems that fire on all cylinders, I was gratified when the lush musicality and quirky imagery of the first few three lines gave way to the rest—no less consonant but with the strand of an argument beginning to come clear. I read in large part for the pleasure of that moment when a pattern begins to emerge— when the pretty crisscrossing lines on a page reveal themselves as a map leading somewhere. In this case, the pattern takes the shape of a downward spiral, from obscurity into clarity and back into darkness and finally into a light that feels cataclysmic, like the dawn of the universe, with "air / rippling, roiling the surface of the world." If I'm unsettled by that first series of tumbling, disconnected images, by the poem's end I am unsettled in a different way. Trivial, man-made mishaps can be named, unlike failures of flesh or machine. It would be comforting to blame random disasters on someone—God as an apprentice calligrapher still perfecting his stroke?—but in life, unlike art, there is no pattern, and the pickup sticks of happenstance make up nothing so comforting as a map.

•

"Bare lists of words are found suggestive to an imaginative and excited mind," Emerson wrote in "The Poet" (1844). The tongue-twisting list that begins "Ox-Head Dot" offers sensual pleasure through its manipulations of the mouth and intellectual engagement through its seemingly associative technique which leads, in lines 4 and 5, to narrative sense. *Oh.* Another list follows, less playful ("what can go wrong"), the items linked through situational irony and alchemical imagery: the "peel[ed] carrots" transform to "bronze slivers," the ruptured kidney becomes a jammed stabilizer, both woman and jet "plunge ... / ... into the darkness" in which a man shouts "'Hyena!'" Suddenly the poem's true subject—language—rises again to the foreground. That scratching sound is made by both the hyena at the door and the pen on paper as they allow this poem its process of becoming. A third list appears now, thesaural, suggestive of the "defects" inherent in any discipline. Yet the narrator's faith in language leads to a burst of light, many lights, in an orgasmic and incantatory ("air, air / rippling, roiling") transformation.

"Ox-Head Dot" echoes Richard Wilbur's "The Writer," another poem about the creative process. The narrator of Wilbur's poem, unwary of failure, marshals an extended metaphor, only to reject suddenly this "easy figure" and force himself toward revision. That poem's "dazed starling" finally seen "clearing the sill of the world" morphs here into "glowing moths loosed into air ... / ... roiling the surface of the world." Bird and insects vanish into the sky, reminding us that true naming, as Emerson insisted, occurs only when the intellect takes direction from the celestial.

•

The list of flaws in calligraphy is wonderful; I always love to see the vocabulary and the "jargon" (in the good old sense) of crafts or groups come into poems. The sound qualities are rich and supple. The poem argues for the awestruck moment when the small, or the dot, even the dot that is a flaw, opens to the whole world of writing (hence the first and last stanzas). However— and this judgment is absolutely a question of poetic orientation and the ethics of poetics—the second and half of the third stanzas overplay the hand considerably. I find it sentimentalizing, self-aggrandizing even, to compare the fraught feelings of failure as one makes a mark on the page to such flaws as in the adjustment of a "gimbal nut" that causes a whole plane to crash. I recognize that this flaw, like the flaw in calligraphy, is a question of *techne*. But this flaw of *techne* is not at all at issue in the other material stanzas 2 and 3: a flaw in someone's body leading suddenly to collapse and probable death, or to the irruption of mental illness. This disproportion is very typical of normative and well-rewarded poems. It is a disproportion of concept for me, an argument fundamentally about metaphor and reality. The *humilitas* ploy that opens this arc of argument is also rather stagy: "I have no names for what can go wrong"— to which my response is, don't be silly, of course you do: the "I" has written the poem and its highly poetic, pressured, last three lines. This is a perfect mainstream poem: finely articulated, rhetorically adept, stagy, and sentimentalizing.

•

I have several names for what can go wrong: tone constrained *(wisp wasp)*, ending boned *(mouse tailed)*, syntax pulled thin over boxlike frame *(boxed-spring)*, teaspoon for stirring in feeling *(sodden branch)*. Even the Pacific Ocean has a bottom, but you'd be hard pressed to get there with even strokes. "A woman collapses / when a tumor in kidney's ruptures." In her kidney's / Collapses /

A tumor / Ruptures / When a woman . . . Ruptures kidney / Her in tumor / When collapses—. *The rapture of the rumor is/as gone missing.* "Fumble, blunder, mistake, fail." *Tumble, sunder, fake, fall.* These are not only my subjects but also practice (makes imperfect). Are they here, though, synonymous? Does the poem allow its error to lead? To rupture? To collapse? To rapture?

> o, head, get me an ox
> an ox and toad
> to pay the toll
> till I get there
> with nary a care

A. E. Stallings

AMATEUR ICONOGRAPHY: RESURRECTION

Jesus is back—he's harvesting the dead.
He's pulling them up out of the dirt like leeks—
By the scruff of the neck, by the wispy hair on the head,
Like bulbs in darkness sallowly starting to grow

From deep down in the earth where the lost things go—
Keys and locks, small change, old hinges, nails.
(That's why the living beseech the dead, who know
Where missing objects lie.) Jesus has a grip

On Adam by the left wrist—he will not slip—
And Eve, by her right. They're groggy and don't
    understand,
They died so long ago. With trembling lip,
Adam surveys the crowds of new people. And Eve

Looks up the emptiness of her limp left sleeve
For the hand that was unforgiven and is no more,
Ages since withered to dust, and starts to grieve
The sinister loss, recalling the heft in that hand

Of the flesh of the fruit, and the lightness at the core.

•

Grief even after Christian resurrection? I love the idea, not believing or wanting insipid sweetness and delight in this world or whatever dimension to come. This poet's just-resurrected Eve, even though groggy, remembers Eden and, it seems, does not regret her disobedient act but insists that what happened to her and Adam—to all of us—was "sinister." (This is the fulcrum word, the word for which the whole poem creates a context.) So, this is a poem with an intriguing given, a story line that holds our bemused attention, and will.

This caveat: I want more power here. The first two lines should read, for example, "Jesus is back, harvesting the dead, / Pulling them up out of dirt like leeks," and the fifth line, "From deep in the earth where lost things go. . . ." Poet, don't let go of this terrific poem just yet. Its theology will deepen as you shape and sound it until not a syllable isn't inevitable.

•

First thought: very simplistic rhyme. Not a bad thing. I like rhyme that is simple and doesn't brag too much. It is a relief. It is the contrast between this poem's smoothness—its oh-so-obvious form—and its subject—the *amateur* iconography—that makes me feel all weird inside. There are parts of this weirdness that I like. I can't decide for the life of me if this poem is meant to parody in form an unconventional and slightly insane painting of some sort, perhaps a religious scene on black velvet bought at a truck stop. In this reading, the form is meant to be as overwrought as the scene in the painting, meant to mock the painting. Or if it is a high-art comment on an unconventional and slightly insane painting of some sort and is hence guilty of a certain snobbism. Or if it is an amateur empathetic identification with the amateur iconography. Or if the painting is some obvious high-art painting and I just don't get the reference. I sort of like being here in the midst of all this confusion, once again wishing that I had the social apparatus—the sort of poet who wrote; the sort of place that might publish it; the sort of reader who might read it—to cling to. But part of me is also scared that I will find out the answer to be one of the first two when I know the author. And then this poem, which I find so weird, will no longer be weird and will just be a little snide.

•

Twentieth-century art historians have debated long and hard about the provenance of this haunting fresco hidden behind the sacristy in the twelfth-century church of San Maurizio outside the Tuscan city of Siena. The lapis lazuli sky, contrasted with the assertive crimsons of the robes worn by Jesus and Adam, is indicative of Chianciano, the master medieval painter who taught Giotto his expressive style. The contorted figures of Adam and Eve are taken directly from Perugino's "Expulsion from the Garden of Eden" found in the upper-left nave of the church of San Francesco in Assisi. The figure of Eve is particularly striking because of her early Raphaelite beauty touched by the sadness of the loss of her arm. The power of this poem is quite evident in the way the poet has captured the subtle sense of loss in the face of this everywoman Eve.

•

Eve saw Adam eyeing the apple and, taller, reached for it and handed it to him—but first she sweetened it with her lips, like any good mate. How then, *this?* Left arm withered, and she not even a southpaw. And lifetimes later my Aunt Betty tries to save me from this sinister plot by tying my left hand behind my back, forcing me to write with my right. Somewhere in the Middle Ages the scriptures got reinterpreted and Eve ("everywoman") became the fall guy. Maybe it was a small price to pay for the sensuous last lines in this poem.

•

The poem is interesting to me in that its jaunty tone is at odds with its formal restraint, though there is a certain relentlessness in the movement of both. I know from the beginning where the poem is going, but then I also know this scene, which was celebrated among the Orthodox as that moment when Christ, dead on Saturday, descended to purgatory to rescue Adam and Eve, and the poem is also relentless in its *reading* of that scene as depicted in this particular painting. I like it; it seems to me in those last lines to become a "revision" of resurrection, where Eve and Adam are anguished in differing ways at being brought back to life, and where Eve cannot forget the original wound, which is a "sinister loss" in its punishment and yet which had that "heft in that hand//Of the flesh of the fruit, and the lightness at the core." A persistence in the delight of the life of the body, so that those last lines in their sensuous weight outweigh the miraculous descent and resurrection. I would like only for the poem to be perhaps more intense, to have more jauntiness of phrase throughout. The first image of the leeks is very good, but the list of what's lost in the earth, "keys" "old hinges" seems a little predictable. "He will not slip" and he "surveys the crowds of new people" also seem okay but not as resonant as they could be.

•

The Poverty of the Poor Farmer
Must Eve forever be deprived of her left hand, electing as she does to mourn the dreaded fruit for the way it felt in her hand and mouth? If so, the Lord does have a grievous task, taking Eve and the husband she did not even choose and standing them there to watch the final accounting. It's as if they are to blame, as if there is no great plot and theater with a prompter sitting in his box to come to our aid when we let out the cry of despair—*"line!"* This poem mostly works, and when it doesn't it is only because seventeen lines in alternating rhyme form a slightly too small

wagon for the Lord to haul around his crop of bulbous eyes in. Then again perhaps a too-full wagon is the perfect counter-weight to this Judgment Day carnage of empty interiors.

O poor Lord, having to be so disappointed, walking along lifting those who fell so short to see if the interment allowed them to find roots and prepare for celestial living. O poor Lord, how we worry thee. If it were not for the poverty of our imag-ination, there could be no such harvesting of places where the dead live. It was that poverty that led and continues to lead us into speculation, believing and refusing to believe. Such poverty grows out of the gift of a basic impasse, an icon that defies critical dissection. Such is the fruit, the marvelous fruit that lifted human eyes into a greater vision, our impoverished ego looking out onto the world, or so it is given to us in Judeo-Christian accounting.

However, this poem is not about believing. It is about a certain absence.

The last line, "Of the flesh of the fruit, and the lightness at the core," announces everyone's grief, the tripartite God for having to maintain a draining patience and ours for what could have been, had the past been different.

The dead laid in narrow cells forever, to paraphrase Gray's "Elegy Written in a Country Church-Yard," but forever is not forever, just as there is no emptiness in Buddhist emptiness. Hui Neng, the sixth patriarch, announced that there is no mirror, to which a whole school of neo-French psychoanalytic critics could never agree. There must be a mirror. Moreover, this reader should not be writing of it. Yet there must be heaven, and as this poem invokes and celebrates incongruities, first for their neces-sary existence, so can the audience here assume that this reader sees this poem as a seriocomic glance at the entry to Paradise. Just imagine the worst Amtrak nightmare of delayed trains and ill-mannered passengers, the indignant and self-righteous right alongside the silent minority, the saints.

As satire, it carries a fear—maybe guilt—about taking on the Lord this way. This hesitancy about the subject produces a child-like wonder in spaces such as the one that describes the grave in the second stanza as "From deep down in the earth where the lost things go—." The place proves itself to be a lost-and-found, as the living ask the dead for the whereabouts of lost things because we know that they know. Or if we are yet unborn, those in the *genuine life* enjoy a blissful omniscience as they amuse themselves by watching us figure out things . . . like the universe and life. The a-b-a-c rhyme pattern enforces the child's voice inside the adult, as the b-c endings accompany the uncertainty in the child's observation of what is a rather ghastly scene, all of which comes to an end in looking at fruit. It is a carnival of corpses and memories of nice things to eat that ends up giving all humanity food poisoning, or so the story goes.

It is a carnival of absences. The poem's success is in the visual conjuring of places left absent by the living and the dead. The spaces we fill when we walk the earth and then lie in it to come to nothing make it seem like a hollow honeycomb in the poet's hands. That is the physical absence, and in the end Eve carves the absence of unfulfilled love, as the Poor Farmer, the Lord, should have made knowledge and love the reward for tasting something so delightful to the hand but so empty inside, that love and not the conditional love with its requirement that we all must die.

Die we must and then be harvested by the Poor Farmer who will take us to Farmer's Market to be displayed for the denizens of the upper universes who rule where there never was and never will be such things as earths and heavens, where there really is nothing. But here we have no nothingness, so. . . .

"Jesus has a grip" and Adam has a "trembling lip" while Eve gets a "limp . . . sleeve."

•

On first reading, I found this poem very attractive; its ambition—both thematically and formally—is immediately impressive and sets it apart from most contemporary poems I see; it's dramatically compelling (calling to mind in its irony

Rilke's "Orpheus. Eurydice. Hermes."); and it has that (for me) irresistible Southern Gothic feel. But with each subsequent reading I felt my affection eroding, and perhaps, given the poem's otherwise obvious successes, it's worth discussing why.

I'll start with the punch line: it is a formal problem. While attempting to write a loosely iambic, rhyming poem and therefore to give the poem a formal dress to wear to its formal occasion, the poet, I believe, has overlooked more important formal concerns: there isn't a moment of syntactic drama or of linguistic excitement that remotely complements the narrative drama of the poem. In fact, the writing is very loose, careless even; the dead-as-leeks simile, for instance, of line 2—a lovely image wonderfully amplified and vivified by "the wispy hair" in line 3—becomes "like bulbs" in line 4. But leeks *are* bulbs, aren't they? Couldn't the "like" have been dropped from the line to create both greater precision and concision? Yes, of course. And so could most of the prepositional phrases be dropped and condensed, thereby energizing the language, but the poet let an ill-conceived notion of form get the better of her or him, and the lack of precision that followed undermines the poem. To my mind, for instance, the "sinister" of the penultimate line is robbed of its potential power because of the sloppiness that precedes it; the play on *sinistre* seems simply clever or precious, since this sort of attention to detail has been lacking in the language of the rest of the poem.

In the ongoing—and mostly stupid—debate between the merits of free and formal verse, this poem provides a good example of how things can go wrong on the formal side: while achieving a superficial formality, this poem has lost its formal integrity. That said—and perhaps oversaid!—I still find this poem genuinely interesting and promising.

Charles Bernstein

every lake has a house
& every house has a stove
& every stove has a pot
& every pot has a lid
& every lid has a handle
& every handle has a stem
& every stem has an edge
& every edge has a lining
& every lining has a margin
& every margin has a slit
& every slit has a slope
& every slope has a sum
& every sum has a factor
& every factor has a face
& every face has a thought
& every thought has a trap
& every trap has a door
& every door has a frame
& every frame has a roof
& every roof has a house
& every house has a lake

•

Let the circle be unbroken—but is it a claddagh or a noose? Someone is caught in a nursery rhyme. She sits by the window in a hard-backed chair, peers out at the lake through a slit in the curtains—and longs for life and longs for death. And all because of one pivotal word that gives this scene an edge.

•

I'd like to teach this poem, but I wouldn't want to read it again. There's a lot to discuss here, as is always the case with poems that have highly theoretical underpinnings. The self-consciousness of the poet, the self-reflexivity of the text—man, I could go on forever, and a class of excitable sophomores would be right there with me. Sooner or later, though, someone would say: "This poet is, like, real smart and everything, but the poem's not very interesting." In defense of my profession, I'd argue with the young upstart, but secretly I'd agree.

•

Yes, this poem harkens back to a nursery song—the one, in particular, that begins: "As I was going to St. Ives / I met a man with seven wives" and ends "Kittens, cats, sacks, wives; / how many were going to St. Ives?" The point of that song—besides the obvious pleasures of rhyme and of bouncy meter—is the end's mathematical riddle. Similarly, the poem before us is all about logic. Apart from its trance-inducing repetition, it eschews poetry's usual pleasures. These images refuse to be particular or sensuous. Instead of a house we can see—weathered clapboards, crumbling chimney—we have a Platonic house, an everyhouse. The poem's movement—from its pared-down domestic imagery to mathematics and full circle back to the daily world—is its point. Familiar objects can be reduced to formula: slope, sum, and factor. This intrigues me. I wonder, though: Does every factor really have a face? Just as any object can be reduced to a formula, does every formula translate back into the physical? I'm willing to buy this, am fascinated by the idea, but am ultimately held at arm's length by the poem's spare structure. I want it to show me—to prove its theories—but in its insistence on the general and on its own relentless forward-marching rhythm, it refuses.

•

While I find this formulaic writing annoying in its presumption of cleverness, I find one respondent's comment even more annoying in its presumption of "highly theoretical underpinnings": "I'd like to teach this poem...man, I could go on forever." Dear God. Even if such underpinnings exist, any engagement would have less to do with the two dozen words—one adjective, one verb, one article (and its variant in line 7) and twenty nouns—that comprise the almost two dozen lines than with the intellect brought to bear upon them. The text becomes no more than an arbitrary scrim through which the mind moves, examining itself. Once the discussion had concluded, the piece still wouldn't be any better. (And *why* does this respondent refer to the narrator as "She"?)

Another respondent notes that the piece "eschews poetry's usual pleasures." Amen. Neither are there unusual pleasures, for that matter.

•

All this discussion begs the questions: What is the occasion of this poem? What are the demands of this poem? And what are we, as readers, demanding from it? This poem is obviously a variation of the list poem, and I'm drawn to its looping, never-ending aspect. My take: this poem begs to be three-dimensional, to be freed from the page and displayed on a ticker or printed on a hula hoop or a necklace or bracelet. I'd be just as happy with any one of the lines opening the poem and any ending it. I'd like "every lake" to be a poem I could enter and leave at any time or even read three or four times in a row, like a nursery rhyme. Every house doesn't have a lake. Every factor doesn't have a face. And I think that these assumptions on the part of the narrator make him or her extremely suspicious and interesting. I think this poem could best be taught by having students "make" it. In other words, what would this poem look like if it existed elsewhere instead of on a flat sheet of paper?

•

All the lines of this jingle are what I. A. Richards called, nonpejoratively, "pseudo-statements." A poem must convince us of its own truths, at least while we are inside it (even if these truths will not bear up against logical scrutiny, against that reality that exists beyond hypnosis and song). "Nature's first green is gold"; "My life closed twice before its close—"; "The world is charged with the grandeur of God"; "That is no country for old men"; "every atom belonging to me as good belongs to you"; "She sang beyond the genius of the sea"; "The whiskey on your breath / Could make a small boy dizzy"; "feeling is first"; "The rose is obsolete"; and so on. This abstracted, playful, circular ramble, though, makes me want to resist and contradict it, line by line, and that's easy enough to do.

I wonder why the poet didn't just write this poem, realize that he or she had something very artificial and slight here, and let it be, unpublished. Sure, we could talk about it for hours, make stories of it, find import in our ingenious professional ways. But what has this to do with the art of high seriousness to which we've devoted our lives?

Miranda Field

IN ORDER TO LOWER
THE FEVER OF FEELING

If the dream is city or elevator, it's easy to mistake
the outer boroughs or lobby for not-dream. But you
have to be excruciatingly awake to know your
otherself is as securely yoked to sleep. The water I'm
waiting in grows colder. In the bath-tub I'm divided
in two, most of me amorphous under the surface.
My thighs and knees and crotch have almost entirely
dissolved, like a watercolor a glass of water has
been knocked across. And that part of me that lies—
reverse *fata morgana*—under the lid of the underwater
sky, is my own but mythical. So if its periscope
could now rise up through the surface, what would
it see? Who bears the weight of being more devotedly:
this lion's share, whom people know by name, or
her far blurrier anchor? But leave us—shy and
shivering conjoined twins—alone. Our sleep is filled
with neither soothing properties nor buoyancy.

•

"In Order to Lower the Fever of Feeling" does what prose
poems do best—inhabit the worlds of prose and poetry, of lyric
and the narrative, offering an anti-epiphany or moral at the end
of the fable. The straddling of above and below, of dream and

nondream, of solid and "amorphous" is brilliantly rendered in the image of looking at the lower half of one's body in a tub as though "a watercolor a glass of water has been knocked across." The "far blurrier anchor" seems to me a metaphor for the prose poem itself, the big block of prose that seems to fasten the poet's loftier musings.

•

Sitting in a cold bath to lower the fever of feeling? This poem is something of a cold bath, too. It is one of many in English about doubleness, dividedness, our intuition that we are not entirely integrated selves—not whole. This was a major theme of Auden's, associated with our "fallen" state. Here the dividedness is between dream and not-dream, sleep and waking, the body below and the body above the surface of the cooling water. I don't know if this body is male, but that phallic periscope, rising even in a cold bath, causes a snicker. Or should I take the "her" in "her far blurrier anchor" to suggest that the body is female and see the periscope merely as one of several mixed metaphors in the poem? Still, the last sentence is striking— are we awake or asleep? It's the one part of the poem that approaches lyric memorability (though Frost's "After Apple Picking," less cerebral, less a cold bath, is more effective for my money).

•

I like the sense of in-betweenness in this poem that extends from writer to reader. Even the sex of the speaker is indeterminate, possessing both a phallic periscope and "her far blurrier anchor." This lyric is not only amorphous but amphibious. Caught between waking life and sleep, between the waters of birth and the watery grave of death, we are suspended within the baptismal element without ever being invited to step out of the font, even as the water "grows colder" entropically. Only the mythic imagination, it seems, can free us from the second law of thermodynamics or at least delay the onset of that final sleep that all of us find ourselves sinking in.

•

"I do not think a merciful Providence meant the 'prose-poem' to last," William Dean Howells wrote to Stephen Crane, though His store of mercy seems to have diminished during the previous century. Poetry must be at least as well written as prose (Pound), but prose must also be as well written as, well, prose, and the ten sentences that constitute this paragraph seem labored, huffing along from "But" to "And" to "So" to "But," the string of conjunctions meant to keep the piece aloft. The language dwells in the rarefied atmosphere of Thought, its heft ("thighs and knees and crotch") less important than its airy discursiveness ("part of me . . . mythical"). It's that lack of attention to "the weight of being," finally, that allows gender to slip from the unintentionally humorous phallic periscope to "her," then to the terrible pun of the final word. With some revision, these sentences might be recast as lines, leaning toward precision and clarity (that contrast with Frost is apt) in their contemplative drift.

•

I love the lyricism of the title. I guess my question of this poem is: What does it want to say that matters? That we need to know? I think the poem says whatever it says with great beauty (I can't hear the huffing; I like conjunctions) but I'm not sure what this is beyond a certain lostness. I keep wanting to make meaning out of the wonderful way the poem begins with the city, the city that is hard to map, and then moves down through the city to one particular bathtub and the hard-to-map and -gender body there. Is there something to be said about the relationship between cities and bodies? I'm not sure what it is yet. My hope, because I find this poem tantalizing, is that there are twenty more parts to it.

Christopher Davis

INCEST

1.
Pretty brother, I belly-
flop onto your grave

and I pray,
"Suffocate

under the weight
of this fat life."

2.
in a fireplace of a chimney made
from headstones, yellow daisies

blaze: later
he takes

a pink teacup rose, balances
it behind his ear: in his brain

a naked boy escapes
his embrace, passes

away to a place
beyond shame:

•

"Incest," as part of a sequence or among other poems by which its suppressions could be made clear, might be memorable, but what is here is not enough. Form may be solace and protection, but *who* is *where* in this construct which seems more clever than necessary? Seventeen long *a* notes hold this two-movement—anger, then italicized resolution—lyric together, and the death-in-birth image of graves-in-hearth pierces, and I may understand that the poem demands its own incestuous secrets, but I want more grounding and less artifice before I can feel the passion in the huge blank space of time beyond the hovering final colon.

•

A poem entitled "Incest" is likely to be playing—already the word "playing" disturbs me—around and against margins, and it is going to be easy for a reader to get caught with a foot in the door that divides ethical and esthetic categories—to mix the metaphors thoroughly. But then I think "Incest" does mix metaphors. It begins with sexuality as metaphor, then moves on to deal with the vehicle only—no, tenor only?—but at any rate, only allows us to see one side of the implied comparison. Someone is comforted, there is a fire in the fireplace, which means home and protection, right?—there is a place beyond shame, which is beyond the colon, beyond the language visible on the page, which is a place where love cannot be damaged or cannot damage, whatever that "love" happens to manifest.

This poem disturbs me, has taken me the longest to talk about, and it just won't go away. It addresses a "pretty brother" who is in a grave. "Belly- / flop" is a highly suggestive if boyishly playful act. The voice commands the brother to suffocate . . . the belly flop can be fatal. Life is fat, is full of matter, of being, of flesh. . . . Above the grace of the grave, there is nothing beyond the connecting punctuation. Below the surface, in the grave, where flesh melts back into origins, maybe there is forgiveness for some sort of sin, or love, which remains nameless. Which cannot speak its name?

·

The place beyond shame is death, which is why I believe the poet ends with a colon reminiscent of Dickinson's dash, to indicate that imminent absence. The first section is both weirdly comic and grotesque: the sexuality behind "pretty brother" is frightening due to the title, and yet the image of belly flopping onto a grave in the hopes of smothering that brother with "this fat life" is nearly impossible for me to treat seriously. (Can anyone use the term "belly-flop" in a poem without making the diction comic?)

The second half of the poem plays far more explicitly on death as a subject: the chimney made of headstones, the daisies, the line break after "passing away," even the relentless keening sound of the repeated "a"s. What I don't emotionally comprehend yet, however, is how I should feel about this boy (brother?) who is dead. Was he the victim of incest? Was he the perpetrator of the incest? Is the "he" the "I" of the first part of the poem? Is the naked boy the "he" or the "I" of the first part? Does the poet mean for such illeist confusion? Why is the naked boy's escape taking place in the brain, not the memory or the imagination ("brain" is such a medical, almost antiseptic word)? And finally, is this a literal incest that has taken place or a metaphorical one? I'm inclined to argue that it must be a literal one, since to use "incest" as a title for a metaphor not only seems incredibly callous but also a cheap way of drawing the reader into the poem with its (implied?) promise of confession. The fact that the "confession" isn't ever explicitly made—at least not according to our notions of confessional writing—is the poem's strongest point, though I still don't know what intellectual or external exploration the poet is trying to make out of the subverted personal narrative.

^•

I believe "Incest" needs to be developed into a longer sequence. The use of couplets in the existing two sections gives the poem a formal unity, and the use of italics in the second section places it in dramatic contrast to the first. Nevertheless, the overall situation needs clarification and intensification. I admire how provocative the first section is, how elliptical the second section is, but I think the colon creates a boomerang effect. Although the poem tries to create an open-ended resonance at the end, it hasn't been earned yet. In section 2, for instance, it's unclear why the yellow daisies "blaze." If the yellow daisies somehow intensify the emotional situation, it's not clear to this reader why or even how they do so.

If the structure of the poem can be thought to resemble a stone-and-gravel garden where the exposed portions of stone interact in a larger field of energy, then more stones (I suspect there are some entirely below surface) need to be partially exposed so that what lies beneath can exert its essential pressure.

•

Many—I'd venture to say most—lyric poems use implied narrative to ground their imagery, to lend weight to their flights of rapture or sorrow. Is the emotion earned? a skeptical reader might ask of any poem that skirts the line between sentiment and sentimentality, and very often the evidence that earns a poem the right to extreme emotion rests in implied narrative. Certainly, this poem couldn't be accused of senti-mentality; the poet admirably aims at restraint, but overshoots. "Incest" not only withholds much of the narrative promised by its incendiary title but also succeeds almost completely in staving off emotion altogether. What narrative we get is sketchy. Physical contact seems to have been initiated by the speaker of the first section. After all, we're told that in the living brother's mind:

> a naked boy escapes
> his embrace, passes
>
> away to a place
> beyond shame:

Is victimization implied? Maybe, if only by the word "escapes." Perhaps that self-conscious ending colon invites me to suppose that the surviving boy feels shame—and yet there's that tonally peculiar opening stanza, suggesting a mix of playfulness and threat. While just such an emotional mix may well exist between brothers, incestuous or not, it doesn't feel like enough to sustain a poem about a charged topic like incest.

•

I probably would not have given so much thought to this poem if I came across it in a magazine. It seems to get all of its kick from the trigger of the title. As far as I am concerned, that *does* amount to sentimentality, if sentimentality is "unearned emotion." There are some phrases/effects of interest ("belly- / flop," the final colon), and which demonstrate a level of skill and sophistication. And maybe, as has been mentioned, the poem succeeds in the context of a larger sequence. But as it stands, the poem wants the readers to do its work for it.

Two takes, from first and third person. It is not clear whether the incest of the title is a real or imagined event, or whether said incest is physical or somehow metaphorical. The chimney made from headstones stumps me. Is this a real chimney, or a description of a monument in a cemetery? Do the daisies blaze simply because of their intense color and the internal rhyme? Or is someone actually cremating the flowers cathartically? Here I am expending more words on this than the poet, and I am no closer.

Denise Duhamel

NOAH AND JOAN

It's not that I'm proud of the fact
that twenty percent of Americans believe
that Noah (of Noah's Ark) was married
to Joan of Arc. It's true. I'll admit it—
Americans are pretty dumb and forgetful
when it comes to history. And they're notorious
for interpreting the Bible to suit themselves.
You don't have to tell me we can't spell anymore—
Ark or Arc, it's all the same to us.

But think about it, just a second, time-line aside,
it's not such an awful mistake. The real Noah's Missis
was never even given a name. She was sort of
    milquetoasty,
a shadowy figure lugging sacks of oats up a plank.
I mean, Joan could have helped Noah build that ark
in her sensible slacks and hiking boots. She was
    good with swords
and, presumably, power tools. I think Noah and Joan
might have been a good match, visionaries
once mistaken for flood-phobic and heretic.

Never mind France wasn't France yet—
all the continents probably blended together,
one big mush. Those Bible days would have been
good for Joan, those early times when
          premonitions
were common, when animals popped up
out of nowhere, when people were getting cured
left and right. Instead of battles and prisons
and iron cages, Joan could have cruised
the Mediterranean, wherever the flood waters
          took that ark.

And Noah would have felt more like Dr. Doolittle,
a supportive Joan saying, "Let's not waste any
          time!
Hand over those boat blueprints, honey!"
All that sawing and hammering would have
          helped
calm her nightmares of mean kings and crowns,
a nasty futuristic place called England.
She'd convince Noah to become vegetarian.
She'd live to be much older than 19, those
          parakeets
and antelope leaping about her like children.

•

If the columnist Dave Barry wrote poetry, it might resemble
"Noah and Joan," the stanzas like tidy paragraphs, the diction
utterly conversational, the whole thing rather like genial prose.

Its geniality disguises a tough-minded vision, of course. Issues of American innocence or dangerous ignorance have a biting currency, and this poem manages to imagine a world in which the disaster of the flood is a kind of salvation, erasing nations and the nationalist squabbles that have turned young people like Joan into soldiers. Death has undone so many at that age—nineteen. It suggests that saving work—carpentry and husbandry—might almost drown out the "nightmares of mean kings and crowns," that organizations like Habitat for Humanity almost succeed. But history has the unspoken last word in the poem. Children grow up and die, and we have not seen the last of "battles and prisons." I like this poem. I wish it had more poetry in it, though, more ore in its rifts, more tension. Like much of the most popular poetry, it just doesn't seem very ambitious. Perhaps that lack of verbal tension is another of the poem's deliberate ironies, a faux-naif quality that lets its dark historical message creep up on us. If I read a whole book of poems like this I would have mixed feelings—admiration and a restless desire for something more memorable.

•

The lazy diction and the sweeping ironies in "Noah and Joan" must be intentional—imitative of the reductive sensibilities of American high school students, presumably, and of an American culture that plays fast and loose with history and the arc of religious faith. Americans, the author acknowledges, "can't spell anymore." Their thinking tends toward "one big mush": the continents are "blended together," time lines are ignored—Joan dressed for her biblical appearance like an L. L. Bean model in "sensible slacks and hiking boots"—and the moral tales of the past are tuned toward new relevancy when Noah becomes a vegetarian. By implication, American writing is also a blend, with the emphasis on today's lingo. What nuance in phrases like "pretty dumb," "such an awful mistake," "sort of milquetoasty," "flood-phobic"? The too-common phrasing, one begins to suspect, is meant to be representative of popular imagination, where "out of nowhere" and "left and right" events of durable interest are glossed over.

For instance, kings are described as being merely "mean" and Joan "could have cruised / the Mediterranean, wherever the flood waters took that ark." The ark, which was originally a saving place for creatures, a metaphor for compassion and procreation, and, more sinister, the last chance for a human race that has disgraced itself in God's eyes, is a linguistic repository too. The poet's language comes in twos—nouns paired, as in the Noah and Joan of the title, "kings and crowns," "parakeets / and antelope"; repetitions, as in "France wasn't France," and "Ark or Arc"; syntactic doubles, as in "She'd convince Noah to become vegetarian. / She'd live to be much older. . . ." It's easy enough to miss—if not entirely subtle—and readers who merely look for the poetry in the poem or for a complement to their high-minded sociopolitical views could end up feeling like the butt of the poet's joke or miss the joke entirely. Whew. Would I have been embarrassed!

•

In "Noah and Joan" what begins as a criticism of American misinformation soon turns into a defense—and for good reason: the subject quickly shifts from "they" to "we" and—lo!—the speaker is one of the "20 percent of Americans" who blur time lines and interpret the Bible to "suit themselves." With the voice and vocabulary of an adolescent and the cunning of a stand-up comic, the poet slyly flattens geography and history into "one big mush" and steers the reader down the healing waters of a new feminist perspective. In the Midrash tradition, the poet uses humor to break gender stereotypes: Joan becomes a cross-dresser with a flair for construction and navigation (though one has to question the wisdom of hiking boots for a Mediterranean cruise) and Noah becomes a mechanically challenged animal-rights activist. The poem could well be retitled "Joan and Noah." So far so good. But what of Noah's nameless wife? In fleshing out her nondescript role by promoting her stand-in, Joan, to senior partner, the poet has relegated the "shadowy figure" to the flooding riverbank. Meanwhile, back at the Ark, Noah—the cad!—has a new French flame! What hath the poet wrought?

•

Of all the poems I've read for this project, this is the one I'd like to read more than once. Whereas so many poems these days just seem like language intelligently (or not so intelligently) organized, this one adds to the store of available reality, as John Berryman would say. It begins with a joke, which is always an effective way to begin, and then it makes the reader look closely at three situations. The first two are historical, more or less, and in these two cases, readers are offered insights into 1) what gender politics were like in the Old Testament; and 2) the kind of mind you need if you're going to be a full-tilt regime-changer like Joan of Arc. And then there's the third, imaginary situation of Noah's and Joan's marriage: more sexual politics, more reformer psychology. Thank you, whoever wrote this, for you have packaged several poems within the skin of one. And instead of tired old clouds and streams and falling leaves, you've actually used original, fresh, never-seen-before images. A joke, some smarts, a fistful of crunchy images: Tell me, what more could a reader desire?

•

This is a poem I would teach to university students unfamiliar with the reading and writing of poetry in order to demonstrate that the medium can envelop a broad spectrum of topic and tone. In other words, poetry can speak about anything and in any manner it wishes to. This poem is funny and it is uplifting. It may even fall into the category of light verse. Whether it is serious literature I do not pretend to know, nor do I think the author cares. Ultimately—and unfortunately—I feel I am not a good reader for this poem because I have become altogether weary of poems based on mythology—comedic or earnestly allusive. But this is my particular allergy and one I could have never acquired without having written several myth-based poems of my own.

•

They could be the couple next door, he the retired bank manager with an interest in boats and she the lifelong scholar-athlete who left the nunnery at eighteen after only a few months, a couple you might expect to have a rather large carpentry project in the commodious range of green that is their oversized but all too American backyard as signature of suburbia. The limitless choices allowed in parts of this culture allow much charm or eccentricity, most charming when it is harmless, as is this lively poem that both satirizes and praises America the unenlightened. "visionaries / once mistaken for flood-phobic and heretic." We are the flood survivors. The flood survivors are us.

The unenlightened are the only ones capable of writing the book on beauty's complexity. "Noah and Joan" begins as an apology for the American preference for not knowing and then moves on to defend that archaic innocence as the poem becomes persona.

"You don't have to tell me we can't spell anymore— / Ark or Arc, it's all the same to us."

Indeed it is. We can blame that on dropping Latin and Greek as doctoral requirements. Cast thine eyes on the wreckage of autodidacts infesting the academy.

Ah, but to wit. ... The four stanzas are built of nine Spenserian lines, and the poem is itself the ark, arcing over a mock-heroic tinge in the writing. Joan goes forth as the Holy Cross knight now wife to a man mad with visions. The poem moves from century to century, culture to culture, setting aside the time line to bring some justification for the fact that 20 percent of Americans believe Joan of Arc was Noah of that Ark's wife. An ark is an arc, after all, no matter whether it once contained the divine contract or not, no matter whether it is enshrouded by the protective skirt of Shekhinah. The fact is that it is not simply a line on Joan's obsessive hubby's blueprints.

Once the poet lets go of any pretense to wanting to remake this embarrassing file in the American population, that unpredictable and dubious fifth column, the humor rolls against the reader as the biblical waves of that global washing and cleansing must have done against Noah's and Joan's inimitable boat. Nothing that has come after that glorious tub has managed to contain all life, with all the trouble involved, even the parakeets and antelope that would surely have kept Joan young. Besides, any woman with equal facility in wielding swords and power tools deserves nothing less. The whir of it is noble.

The preponderance of bubbly and perky consonantal "b"s and "p"s add to the busy quality of the boat and its captain with his now-all-too-public wife. There is only the creak and moan of the planks under the weight of the world's beasts to mourn her loss of anonymity.

"She'd convince Noah to become vegetarian." No "p"s there, but the point is made. "Convince" has its own consonantal umph.

The poem allows us a space to laugh at it and ourselves. The letting-go is infectious, kept, as it is, in a neoformalist mode. Living in her husband's time instead of her own, Joan would have been humbled and thus saved from martyrdom by the daily occurrence of miracles. There was one continent, one consequence of God's breath, and the oceans more the overarching canvas of a plum around what once attached it to a tree.

"Joan could have cruised / the Mediterranean, wherever the flood waters took that ark . . . parakeets / and antelope leaping about her like children."

Ah Joan, you have defied or is it that you have made an arc over the ark of these stanzas like hulls, these lines like planks signed by the way wood grows and is thus stamped by knots. Thou shalt not be funny is here the commandment beautifully broken.

Steady at the helm, Joan. You know Noah is a lousy driver.

•

Juxtaposition is integral to poetry, as the French Surrealists discovered, and to the telling of jokes, as comedians know. The joke in this poem is that there *is* a connection between Noah and Joan of Arc: in Christian theology the Old Testament prefigures the Gospels, the new covenant fulfills the promise of the old, the Church is an ark for the faithful, and Noah may be viewed as a model or type for a Christian saint like Joan of Arc, a believer heeding the word of God in an attempt to save Creation. The flood that Noah and the animals survived represents an altogether different order of catastrophe from the issues— territorial, dynastic, and religious—involved in the Hundred Years War, although the voices heard by the Maid of Orléans counseling her to take up arms against the English suggest more of an affinity with the vengeful God of the Old Testament than with the love proclaimed by Christ Jesus. And the poet's recognition of a linguistic connection between Ark and Arc is profound, notwithstanding its origin in the general ignorance of history displayed by the American people: the aesthetic arc of a poem traces the outline of an ark for our emotional lives. The poet Mark Strand observed that Nabokov's lovely phrase *spatial memory* might have derived from a misprint for *special memory*, for it is the writer's obligation to seize on those coincidences, puns, and slips of the tongue by which the world of analogy is revealed. In such a world, which is sometimes described in the most prosaic terms, as in this poem, Noah and Joan of Arc might fall in love and save each other. Is there any other world?

David Mason

A FLOAT

Flotsam? Jetsam? I don't know.
Not dropped from the jet stream
but floated from the Sea of Japan,
a glass float lost
by a village fisherman.

By the time I picked it up
in someone's summer house
it had already been found
on a Puget Sound beach.
The foundling I discovered was not lost

but left on a what-not shelf
among the paperbacks. I held the old
salty ball of glass ridged for a net
(that was not there) to catch
the long-gone fish.

The fisherman who lost it must
also be lost. The friend
whose house I did not find it in—
lost too in the sense
that dead people are

outlasted by a frosty glass ball
among the dog-eared book jackets,
but not bested, not blasted.
Netless, maybe. Uncaught,
unreachable in this room.

•

Unlike "Conduit," which glides gracefully through many
scenes, "A Float" snags on my desire for narrative meaning. But
when I skim the surface, I'm confused. There are so many peo-
ple and places not here. Somehow, I feel they must mesh, but I
can't seem to tie them together. There's the fisherman who
"must / . . . be lost." (Why? Is it because he lost the float?)
There's the friend "whose house I did not find it in." (Who? Not
the owner—the summerhouse where the speaker picks up the
float belongs to "someone.") The friend is dead, in another
house. Is this his/her elegy? What's the connection between the
dead friend and the float? A poem must weave a stronger net—
or else go netless, moving freely through the ocean. For me, "A
Float" depends on surface tensions: "jetsam"/"jet stream," "not
dropped . . . but floated," "The foundling I discovered was not
lost," "not bested, not blasted." These sound and word games
keep the poem "afloat" and make depths truly unreachable.

•

The game's afoot in "A Float," and the game appears to be about
identification and negation, knowing by not knowing. The lost
float's finder can't know whether it was flotsam (found floating)
or jetsam (jettisoned from a distressed ship), or both, especially
when it's found secondhand, on a "what-*not* shelf." Once dis-

covered, the lost thing becomes found, at least to the finder. For the imagined village fisherman (surely a romantic view of those gargantuan Japanese fishing fleets with nets the size of Ohio) the float is still lost, and the fisherman is lost to the speaker, as is the dead friend—unreachable and uncaught in the poem's room.

•

Very straightforward elegiac poem of the memento-mori ilk. Formal in its appropriately humanistic cinquains with a nice looseness in its varied line lengths. The salty ball of glass is a veritable Urim and Thummim. What is not caught, not reachable, remains for us as readers to complete.

•

What matters . . . wordplay in the flotsam, jetsam, jet stream; bested, blasted, netless. I love the play in this poem between the found and the lost, between the known and the unknown, between tightness and looseness of form. And I value its dedication to imagined connections. It is an elegy for those known and not known. I have no problem following the poem—it moves like the glass float caught in the currents.

•

"A Float" is an example of a ubiquitous poem type, the one that begins with a casual discovery and slowly works its way up to king-sized statements—in this case, about the limits that the physical world places on us. What might make this process of discovery more engaging is a sense of the poet's eagerness to probe and learn. There's a stoic, almost anesthetized feeling here; this is as quiet a poem as I've read in months. I felt obliged to supply my own enthusiasm, which is something the poet shouldn't leave up to the reader's discretion.

•

This poem, five lines by five stanzas or a cinquain squared, with an allegorizing pun about the tone and mood given in the title, shows me that a poem can be pallid even when it has a fairly lively use of one formal/modal feature of a poetic text— in this case, sound. The first two stanzas and the last stanza are interestingly rich in sound, cast in a meditative, colloquial, self-questioning voice that nonetheless loses its syntactic bearings and diminishes into filler in the middle of the poem. The sound is most aggressive in the first and last—with the fl/fs, st/ts, and ls combinations in "flotsam"/"jetsam," "float"/"lost," and in the last stanza: "outlasted," "frosty," "glass," "jackets," "bested," "blasted," "netless." The sound in stanza 2 is assonance—the "ou" of "house," "found," "sound," "foundling." Actually, this makes the word "outlasted" in stanza 5 what I call a "pool word"—a word that collects sounds important to the poem but a word that also makes a thematically relevant statement. Withal, I find this poem a bit forced. Not, I hasten to add, because of the sound (hardly) but because some of the imagery is decorative: the "jet stream" of stanza one comes into the poem just for the "j" sounds and the distortion of "jetsam"—really odd to think of any object's being "dropped from the jet stream" (get real!), and the same is true of "foundling," which adds only sound, not useful imagery. The poem is quite familiar and tired out in its subject stance, the "I" taking up this "memento mori" and examining it, a Yorick's-skull kind of move. Alas, poor poem, I knew it well.

Paisley Rekdal

STRAWBERRY

I am going to fail.
I'm going to fail cartilage and plastic, camera
 and arrow.
I'm going to fail binoculars and conjugations,
all the accompanying musics: *I am failing,*
I must fail, I can fail, I have failed
the way some women throw themselves
into lover's arms or out trains,
fingers crossed and skirts
billowing behind them. I'm going to fail
the way strawberry plants fail,
have dug down hard to fail, shooting
brown runners out into silt, into dry gray beds,
into tissue and rock. I'm going to fail
the way their several hundred hearts below surface
have failed, thick, soft stumps desiccating
to tumors, the way roots wizen in the cold
and cloud black, knotty as spark plugs, cystic
synapses. I'm going to fail light and stars and tears.
I'm going to fail the way cowards only wish they
 could fail, the way
the brave refuse to fail or the fain fear to,
believing that to stray even once from perfection
is to be permanently cast out, Wandering Jew
of failure, Adam of failure, Sita of failure; that's the way
I'm going to fail, bud and creosote and cloud.

I'm failing pet and parent. I'm failing the food
in strangers' stomachs, the slender, inchoate rings
of distant planets. I'm going to fail these words
and the next and the next. I'm going to fail them,
I'm going to fail her—trust me, I've already failed him—
and the possibility of a *we* is going to sink me
like a bad boat. I'm going to fail the way
this strawberry plant has failed, alive without bud,
without fruit, without tenderness, hugging itself
to privation and ridiculous want.
I'm going to fail simply by standing in front of you,
waving my arms in your face as if hailing a taxi:
I'm here, I'm here, please don't forget me
though you already have, I smell it, even cloaked
with soil, sending out my slender fingers for you,
sending out all my hair, and tongue, and brain.
I'm going to fail you
just as you're going to fail me,
urging yourself further down to sediment
and the tiny, trickling filament of damp;
thirsty, thirsty, desperate to drown
if even for a little while, if even for once:
to succumb, to be destroyed, to die completely,
to fail the way I've failed:
in every particular sense of myself,
in every new and beautiful light.

•

As an anaphora-driven and cataloging poem, this poem gathers its momentum from a verbal insistence working in tension with a certain disjunctiveness and surprise at the level of detail. The poet does a good job of working his repetitions without stiffening the rhetoric, so that the poem breathes both rhythmically and syntactically, deriving its emotive power from a certain scope, an expansiveness designed to embody the enormity of failure and the play of the obsessive mind at its excited pitch. While such a poem requires a plenitude to reach its full effect, it likewise risks losing energy as a result, since the details can, if too merely disjunct, begin to feel arbitrarily and superficially ordered and hence cease to raise (and in the process, possibly to break) expectations.

The initial list, "cartilage and plastic, camera and arrow," announces to us that there is an explosive sensibility here, one that resists the orderliness of a clear and linear logic. Details insist on their individual identities, on their failure to connect, on, in the poem's words, "every particular sense of myself." Yes, the word "camera" picks up some resonance with "binoculars" in the next line, which in turn speaks, possibly with the idea of speculative language, to "conjugations," but the prevailing sense is that the poem resists subtextual conversations of this sort. The effect is one of haste, of spiritual and physical breakdown. And the poet's dependence falls heavily on the intrinsic power of the parts, which are often wonderful: in particular that sense of failure in the way "women throw themselves / into lover's arms or out trains." Indeed, the poem has much of the same sense of desperation, the same sense of a world as impassioned and dangerous.

The wit and refreshing voice of lines such as "trust me, I've already failed him" do much to keep the poem lively and engaging. Also the poem's self-deprecations turn credibly to anger and the delightful and mock self-grandeur of "Wandering Jew / of failure, Adam of failure, Sita of failure." I'm not sure the poem is best served, however, by bringing the strawberry plant in twice (and with less dynamism the second time), though I realize the shatter of the strawberry root becomes an organizing image for the movement of the poem. And given the discontinuities of the poem, a lot of weight rests on the final line, which serves as a force of unification. The rhetorical and conceptual energy of "new and beautiful" is okay but a bit anticlimactic, in spite of its sense of ironic reversal.

•

"Strawberry" has the kind of power and vitality that draws me back to Theodore Roethke's poems which evoke the hot earthy sensuality of his greenhouse. The insistent tone of obsessive tension is much akin to Anne Sexton's "awful rowing towards God," and it is this energy that makes this poem one to remember. Word up!

•

This is a stunning poem. The women throwing themselves into lover's arms or out trains in particular haunts me. I wish it didn't. I wish I didn't have to be so mesmerized by the way women fail. And that gets at this poem for me. The poem actually scares me. It is a chant to failing. And it has all the luminous power of a chant—mind-changing metaphors full of as much depth as the strawberry's root system, depth that is both surface and beneath, and also history, with Wandering Jew, Adam, Sita. I kept thinking how much more useful and less scary this poem would be if it was to a word other than "fail." If it was a chant to something else. Not necessarily something all goody-goody and happy but just something that wasn't failure. I'm scared of this poem because I am scared it will make me want to fail. Poetry is powerful. Poetry that works as chant is even more powerful. Metaphors enter deep into our brains and change us in ways we don't really consciously acknowledge. Why does the poet want to tell us this so powerfully?

•

The litany of sins in a confessional might sound like this, were each sin not prefaced with a plea for absolution. But failure here becomes a point of pride. The tone is self-congratulatory. This poem reminds me of the old joke about the superstitious patriarch who, afraid to count his blessings, points to each of his twelve children gathered at the dinner table and says, "Don't count one, don't count two, don't count three. . . ." Where there's no discernible boasting, there's no *mal occhio*. A bit of duplicity? The speaker in the poem fails everything to fail nothing. No expectations, therefore no disappointments. Then any success, no matter how small, will loom large. Not small, however, is the poet's breathtaking skill. *There, there.*

•

I like the risk this poem takes and its ironic celebration of failure. The disjunctive elements "cartilage and plastic, camera and arrow" create a sensibility that is an intersection of fear and desire, yet the natural elements—"the way strawberry plants fail"—and human elements—"the way some women throw themselves / into lover's arms or out trains"—grant an impassioned vitality to the poem. And it's interesting how, by the middle of the poem, the failure feared and yet confronted becomes a kind of virtue, "the way cowards only wish they could fail" or "the brave refuse to fail," so that the quality of failure becomes nearly sacred, a kind of largeness of engagement and risk that few can confront. So there is much that I like and commend in this poem. Having said that, I feel that the ending is perhaps unearned or perhaps aspires too much to the epiphanic. The misstep seems to begin with the repetition of the strawberry plant, as if the poem were restarted or revved up again at that point. I would be tempted to take that section out and have the poem go from "the possibility of a *we* is going to sink me / like a bad boat" directly to "I'm going to fail simply by standing in front of you," and then have the poem end with the strawberry plant section like this:

and the tiny, trickling filament of damp;
thirsty, thirsty, desperate to drown, alive without bud,
without fruit, without tenderness, hugging itself
to privation and ridiculous want.

So that the strawberry plant is there again, but evoked, rather than repeated. My argument for this reading of the poem is its scale, which is viewed as if lens that moves closer and yet perceives on a smaller scale. For the poem begins abstractly and generally with its "musics" and "conjugations," then moves to the "women" and "strawberry plants," then to "bud" and the "food / in strangers' stomachs," then "them," "her," and "him," then "you," so that the focus is continually coming into focus. The larger gesture and claim at the end seem not as convincing as the energy and risk that drives the poem.

•

It all depends on what you mean by failure, what you want from success, and what you imagine poems do. Insofar as this is a successful poem, it fails to fail, but, in failing to fail, it also succeeds at failing. That's a lose-lose scenario (which in the alchemy of poetry we imagine as win-win). The failure of "Strawberry" is that it is an idea dressed in a metaphor rather than a formal or stylistic experience. This gives the piece its charm but also its contained, ironic tone. The poem fails to fail to draw empathy, and, once drawn, twice shy. It's likeable, but maybe more as glad handing than as exchange. "Strawberry" courts then skirts the poetic tropes of failure—of the flaw, blemish, irregular, unfinished, misshapen, misbegotten. Ostensibly about failure, it's curiously incurious about failure's textures and tourniquets, its sting, its song.

ABOUT THE PARTICIPANTS

SUSAN AIZENBERG is the author of *Muse* (Crab Orchard Poetry Series/Southern Illinois University Press, 2002), winner of the Larry Levis Prize from Virginia Commonwealth University for best first or second collection of poetry, and *Peru (Take Three:2*: AGNI New Poets Series, Graywolf Press, 1997); and editor, with Erin Belieu, of *The Extraordinary Tide: New Poetry by American Women* (Columbia University Press, 2001). She is currently Assistant Professor of Creative Writing and English at Creighton University in Omaha, Nebraska.

CHARLES BERNSTEIN teaches at the University of Pennsylvania and is the author of numerous books of poetry, including *Dark City* and *Rough Trades*, and of criticism, including *A Poetics* and *My Way*.

MICHELLE BOISSEAU teaches at the University of Missouri, Kansas City, and is the author of *No Private Life, Understory* (University of Arkansas Press, winner of the 1996 Morse Poetry Prize), and *Trembling Air* (University of Arkansas Press, 2003).

BRUCE BOND'S books of poetry include *Cinder* (Etruscan Press), *The Throats of Narcissus* (University of Arkansas), *Radiography* (Ornish Award, BOA), *The Anteroom of Paradise* (Colladay Award, QRL), and *Independence Days* (R. Gross Award). He has received fellowships from the National Endowment for the Arts, the Texas Commission on the Arts, and other organizations. He is Professor of English at the University of North Texas and Poetry Editor for *American Literary Review*.

PHILIP BRADY'S latest book is *To Prove My Blood: A Tale of Emigrations & the Afterlife* (Ashland Poetry Press, 2003). His books of poetry are *Weal* (Snyder Prize, Ashland, 2000) and *Forged Correspondences* (New Myths, 1996). His work has appeared in *Poetry Northwest, Laurel Review, Poet Lore, Massachusetts Review, College English,* and many other journals. Coeditor of *Critical Essays on Joyce's Portrait,* and Poetry Editor of *Artful Dodge,* he teaches at Youngstown State University, where he directs the Poetry Center.

STEPHEN BURT'S first book of poetry, *Popular Music,* won the Colorado Prize for 1999; his second, *Parallel Play,* will appear from Graywolf in 2005. He has also published a book of criticism, *Randall Jarrell and His Age* (2002), and various essays and reviews. He teaches at Macalester College in St. Paul, Minnesota.

NICK CARBÓ is the author of two books of poetry, *El Grupo McDonald's* (1995) and *Secret Asian Man* (2000). He is the editor of three anthologies of Filipino and Filipino American writing, *Returning A Borrowed Tongue* (1996), *Babaylan* (2000), and *Pinoy Poetics* (2004). He has been awarded fellowships in poetry from the National Endowment for the Arts and New York Foundation for the Arts.

For the last decade, DAVID DANIEL has been Poetry Editor of *Ploughshares* and has taught literature and poetry writing at Emerson College in Boston. His first full-length collection, *Seven-Star Bird,* was published by Graywolf Press in 2003. His poems, essays, and reviews have appeared widely. Daniel is also President and Cofounder of the first independent part-time faculty union in the East—the Affiliated Faculty of Emerson College. For the next year he is touring the country with his book and, occasionally, his band of Nashville Cats, LoveStar.

CHRISTOPHER DAVIS'S first poetry collection, *The Tyrant of the Past and the Slave of the Future,* won the Associated Writing Programs Award for Poetry; his second, *The Patriot,* was published in 1998 by the University of Georgia Press. He teaches at the University of North Carolina at Charlotte.

DENISE DUHAMEL is the author of thirteen books and chapbooks, the most recent of which is *Queen for a Day: Selected and New Poems* (University of Pittsburgh Press, 2001). An Assistant Professor at Florida International University in Miami, she coedited, with Nick Carbó, *Sweet Jesus: Poems about the Ultimate Icon* (Anthology Press, 2002).

RACHEL BLAU DUPLESSIS is the author of *Drafts 1–38, Toll* (2001) from Wesleyan University Press, and *Genders, Races and Religious Cultures in Modern American Poetry* (2001) from Cambridge University Press. She is a poet-critic who teaches at Temple University.

MIRANDA FIELD was born and raised in London, England. She has won a "Discovery"/*The Nation* Award and a Pushcart Prize, and her first book, *Swallow* (Mariner Books, 2002), won a Katharine Bakeless Nason Literary Publication Prize in poetry. She lives in New York City with her husband and two children.

ANNIE FINCH'S books of poetry include *Calendars* (Tupelo, 2003), *Eve* (Story Line, 1997), and the forthcoming *Encyclopedia of Scotland* (Salt Publishing). Her translation of Louise Labé's *Complete Poems* is forthcoming from the University of Chicago Press, her poetry-writing textbook, *A Poet's Craft,* from Eighth Mountain Press, and her collection of essays, *The Heart of Poetry,* in the Poets on Poetry series from University of Michigan Press. She currently teaches in the Graduate Creative Writing Faculty at Miami University.

CAROL FROST'S books include *Pure* (1994), *Venus & Don Juan* (1996), *Love & Scorn,* her new and collected poems (2000), from Northwestern University Press, which was a Poetry Book Club selection (Academy of American Poets) in July 2000, and *I Will Say Beauty* (2003). She is a recipient of two National Endowment for the Arts fellowships and three Pushcart prizes. Presently she teaches at Hartwick College in upstate New York, where she directs the Catskill Poetry Workshop.

DIANE GLANCY teaches Native American Literature and Creative Writing at Macalester College in St. Paul, Minnesota. She received the 2003 Juniper Poetry Prize from the University of Massachusetts Press for *Primer of the Obsolete.* Another collection of poems, *The Shadow's Horse,* was published by the University of Arizona Press in 2003. Glancy also published *Stone Heart: A Novel of Sacajawea* (Overlook Press), in 2003. A new collection of essays, *Geographies of Language,* is forthcoming from the University of Arizona Press.

WILLIAM HEYEN, born in Brooklyn, New York, in 1940, is the author of *Erika: Poems of the Holocaust, Crazy Horse in Stillness* (winner of 1997's Small Press Book Award for Poetry), and many other books. He recently edited *September 11, 2001: American Writers Respond* (2002) for Etruscan Press, which also published his collection of poems, *Shoah Train* (2003). Several new collections will soon appear from MAMMOTH Books including *The Rope: Poems, The Hummingbird Corporation: Stories,* and *Home: Autobiographies, Etc.*

HONORÉE FANONNE JEFFERS is the author of two books of poetry, *The Gospel of Barbecue* (Kent State, 2000), which won the Wick Poetry Prize and was a finalist for the Paterson Poetry Prize, and *Outlandish Blues* (Wesleyan University Press, 2003).

DAVID KIRBY is the Robert O. Lawton Distinguished Professor of English at Florida State University. His poetry was chosen for both *Best American Poetry 2000* and *Best American Poetry 2001* as well as *Pushcart Prize 2001*. His previous collection, *The House of Blue Light,* was published in Louisiana State University Press's Southern Messenger Series, and the same series recently published his new collection, *The Ha-Ha.*

APRIL LINDNER, author of the poetry collection *Skin,* which received the 2002 Walt McDonald First Book Prize from Texas Tech University Press, also has published two scholarly monographs, *Dana Gioia* and *New Formalists of the American West,* in Boise State University Press's Western Writers Series. Her poems have appeared in numerous journals, including *Paris Review, Prairie Schooner, Crazyhorse,* and *The Formalist.* She teaches creative writing at Saint Joseph's University in Philadelphia.

TIMOTHY LIU teaches at William Paterson University. His books of poetry include *Vox Angelica* (1992), *Burnt Offerings* (1995), *Say Goodnight* (1998), and *Hard Evidence* (2001). He edited *Word of Mouth: An Anthology of Gay American Poetry* (2000).

CATE MARVIN'S first book, *World's Tallest Disaster,* was selected by Robert Pinsky for the 2000 Kathryn A. Morton Prize and published in 2001 by Sarabande Books. In 2002 she won the Kate Tufts Discovery Award. She is an assistant professor in English at the College of Staten Island, City University of New York.

DAVID MASON'S books of poems include *The Buried Houses, The Country I Remember,* and a new book, *Arrivals.* Coeditor of several anthologies, he has also published a book of essays, *The Poetry of Life and the Life of Poetry.* He teaches at the Colorado College and lives in the mountains outside Colorado Springs.

CHRISTOPHER MERRILL'S books include four collections of poetry, *Brilliant Water, Workbook, Fevers & Tides,* and *Watch Fire,* for which he received the Peter I. B. Lavan Younger Poets Award from the Academy of American Poets; translations of Aleš Debeljak's *Anxious Moments* and *The City and the Child;* several edited volumes; and three books of nonfiction, including *The Grass of Another Country: A Journey through the World of Soccer.* He directs the International Writing Program at the University of Iowa.

CAROL MOLDAW is the author of three books of poetry: *The Lightning Field* (Oberlin College Press, 2003), winner of the FIELD Poetry Prize, *Chalkmarks on Stone* (La Alameda Press, 1998), and *Taken from the River* (Alef Books, 1993), as well as a chapbook, *Through the Window* (La Alameda Press, 2001). Moldaw's work has appeared widely in journals, including *Antioch Review, Chicago Review, New Republic, Paris Review,* and *Parnassus.* She lives in Pojoaque, New Mexico.

BIN RAMKE edits a poetry series for the University of Georgia Press and edits the *Denver Quarterly* at the University of Denver, where he teaches in the Writing Program. His eighth book of poems, *Matter,* will be published by the University of Iowa Press in 2004.

PAISLEY REKDAL is the author of a book of essays, *The Night My Mother Met Bruce Lee* (2000 and 2002), and two books of poems, *A Crash of Rhinos* (2000) and *Six Girls without Pants* (2003). She has received fellowships from the National Endowment for the Arts, the Fulbright Foundation and the Wyoming Arts Council. She teaches at the University of Utah.

REBECCA SEIFERLE'S third new poetry collection, *Bitters* (Copper Canyon, 2001), won the Western States Book Award and a Pushcart Prize. She is also the author of *The Music We Dance To* (Sheep Meadow, 1999), poems from which won the Hemley Award from the Poetry Society of America and were included in *Best American Poetry 2000.* Her new translation of Cesar Vallejo's *The Black Heralds* is forthcoming from Copper Canyon in Fall 2003. She is the founding editor of www.thedrunkenboat.com, an online magazine.

JULIANA SPAHR was born in Chillicothe, Ohio, and currently lives in Honolulu, Hawaii. Her books include *Fuck You—Aloha—I Love You* (Wesleyan University Press, 2001), *Everybody's Autonomy: Connective Reading and Collective Identity* (University of Alabama Press, 2001), and *Response* (Sun & Moon Press, 1996). She coedits the journal *Chain* with Jena Osman (archive at http://www.temple .edu/chain). She frequently self-publishes her work at http://www2.hawaii .edu/~spahr.

A. E. STALLINGS is an American poet residing in Athens, Greece. Her first collection, *Archaic Smile,* won the 1999 Richard Wilbur Award. Her work has received a Pushcart Prize and twice appeared in the *Best American Poetry* series (1994, 2000). She is currently completing a verse translation of Lucretius' *De rerum natura* for Penguin Classics.

ARTHUR SZE is the author of seven books of poetry, including *The Redshifting Web: Poems 1970–1998* (Copper Canyon Press, 1998) and *The Silk Dragon: Translations from the Chinese* (Copper Canyon, 2001). He lives in Santa Fe, New Mexico, and teaches at the Institute of American Indian Arts.

GLORIA VANDO'S books include *Shadows and Supposes* (Arte Publico Press, 2002), winner of the 2003 Poetry Book Award (Latino Literary Hall of Fame) and the Alice Fay Di Castagnola Award (Poetry Society of America); *Promesas: Geography of the Impossible* (Walt Whitman finalist, Thorpe Menn Book Award winner); and *Caprichos.* Vando is editor of the *Helicon Nine Reader* and coeditor of *Spud*

Songs: An Anthology of Potato Poems. She is Publisher/Editor of Helicon Nine Editions and Cofounder of The Writers Place, a literary center in Kansas City.

MICHAEL WATERS teaches at Salisbury University in Maryland and at the New England College MFA Program in Poetry. His books of poetry include *Parthenopi: New and Selected Poems* (2001) and *Green Ash, Red Maple, Black Gum* (1997) from BOA Editions, and *Bountiful* (1992), *The Burden Lifters* (1989), and *Anniversary of the Air* (1985) from Carnegie Mellon University Press. He has coedited *Contemporary American Poetry* (Houghton Mifflin, 2001) and *Perfect in Their Art: Poems on Boxing from Homer to Ali* (Southern Illinois University Press, 2003).

AFAA MICHAEL WEAVER (b. Michael S. Weaver) is the author of nine collections of poetry and several plays. His latest book of poems is *Multitudes* (Sarabande Books, 2000). He is the Alumnae Professor of English at Simmons College. His Chinese name is Wei Yafeng. He lives in Somerville, Massachusetts.

PERMISSIONS

ABOUT THE MODERATOR

H. L. HIX'S recent books include a collection of essays on poetry, *As Easy As Lying*, published in 2002 by Etruscan, a poetry collection, *Surely As Birds Fly*, published in 2002 by Truman State University Press, and a book of criticism, *Understanding William H. Gass*, published in 2002 by the University of South Carolina Press. He is Vice President for Academic Affairs at the Cleveland Institute of Art.